# The Role of Airpower in the Iran-Iraq War

*by*

RONALD E. BERGQUIST, Maj, USAF
*Research Associate*
Airpower Research Institute

*Air University Press*
*Maxwell Air Force Base, Alabama 36112-5532*

December 1988

**Library of Congress Cataloging-in-Publication Data**

Bergquist, Ronald E.
    The role of airpower in the Iran-Iraq War.

    "December 1988."
    Bibliography; p. 87
    1. Iraqi-Iranian conflict 1980-      —Aerial operations.
    I. Title.
    DS 318.85.B47      1988      955'.054                88-7512

ISBN 1-58566-023-X

First Printing December 1988
Second Printing December 1990
Third Printing February 1998
Fourth Printing January 1999
Fifth Printing October 2000
Sixth Printing October 2001

### Disclaimer

For Sale by the Superintendent of Documents
US Government Printing Office
Washington, DC 20402

# Contents

# About the Author

Maj Ronald E. Bergquist was assigned by Headquarters United States Air Force in August 1981 to be the Air Staff's research associate at the Airpower Research Institute for the 1981–82 year. A career air intelligence officer, he came to Maxwell from duties as a Middle East intelligence analyst in the Regional Estimates Division of the Assistant Chief of Staff, Intelligence, Headquarters USAF. Previous assignments included tours as a watch officer at the 20th NORAD Region, Fort Lee Air Force Station, Virginia; squadron and wing intelligence officer duties with the 45th Tactical Reconnaissance Squadron, Bergstrom AFB, Texas, and the 366th Tactical Fighter Wing, Da Nang Air Base, Vietnam; and as a targeteer at Seventh Air Force headquarters, Saigon, Vietnam. The son of a US Air Force chief master sergeant, Major Bergquist was born in Idaho and raised in Hawaii, Delaware, and Texas. He received his BA in geography and his commission through the Reserve Officer Training Corps (ROTC) at the University of Texas in 1968. He received his MA in Middle East studies from the Naval Postgraduate School in Monterey, California, in 1978. Major Bergquist is also an honor graduate of the Defense Language Institute in the Arabic language and a graduate of the Air Command and Staff College, class of 1982.

# *Preface*

This report is an outgrowth of questions raised in the fall of 1980 and spring of 1981 about the conduct of air operations in the war between Iran and Iraq. Unlike previous Middle Eastern wars, this one had continued over a protracted period while we in the United States and in the US Air Force had been able to observe it only from a distance. As the war haltingly progressed, we began to have a fair picture of what was going on in the air war, though our information was far from complete or detailed. The sketchy picture that emerged, however, seemed to indicate the combatants were using their airpower assets in ways contrary to our expectations. Most notably, it seemed that both sides seemed content *not* to use their airpower and relied instead on ground forces for most combat operations. This report examines the air war between Iran and Iraq, but rather than attempt simply to lay out *what* happened in the war, it attempts to discern *why* Iran and Iraq used their airpower as they did. The results of this study do not call into question any basic US Air Force airpower approaches, but they do highlight significant considerations that affect the use of airpower by Third World nations.

Although the analysis and conclusions in this study are the responsibility of the author alone, it could not have been written without the generous assistance of many individuals. Special thanks must go to Maj Gen John Marks for nominating me to write this report and especially to the men of the Regional Estimates Division, AF/IN—Majs Harry Colestock, Rick L'Heureux, and David Prevost—for ably taking up the slack during my absence from that organization. I must also mention my thanks to the members of the Airpower Research Institute for their guidance, insight, and good humor. Most notably, I must thank Col Kenneth J. Alnwick, Lt Col Don Baucom, Maj George Orr, Capt Brian Cioli, and Capt Harbert Jones. John Schenk and Dot McCluskie kept me from egregious errors of syntax, grammar, and organization. But no matter how much guidance, direction, or inspiration went into this study, it could not have seen the light of day without the untiring efforts of those indefatigable decipherers of my indescribable scrawlings—Jo Ann Perdue, Edna Davis, Marcia Williams, and Connie Smith.

RON BERGQUIST

# Introduction

"The war, they believe, will be won in the air." This statement was the opinion of military analysts in Washington and Western Europe as reported by Drew Middleton in the 5 October 1980 issue of the *New York Times*. The Iran-Iraq war had begun almost two weeks prior when the Iraqi Air Force launched airstrikes on 10 Iranian airfields. Since that time, pictures of smoke billowing from bombed oil facilities in both countries had become a staple on television news programs. Yet, the air war did not seem to be progressing in a "rational" manner. "The failure of both sides to use their air forces in support of ground advances [was] inexplicable to western military sources."[1] By the end of the year, "the Iraqi-Iranian war began to resemble a grappling match between the slow and the disorganized . . . military observers were entertained by the ineptitude of the combatants."[2] And now, two years later, the Iraqis have been forced to withdraw from virtually all occupied territory by a combination of Iranian infantry and artillery attacks. As it turned out, Iranian airpower was not the impetus behind Iranian advances nor was Iraqi airpower any barrier to them.

The Iran-Iraq war has been a unique Third World conflict—two countries with large, relatively untested military forces; well equipped with the best Western and Soviet arms; slugging it out in isolation over an extended period. And one of the most puzzling of its unique characteristics has been the relatively ineffectual use of airpower displayed by both sides. US airmen have been mystified about the conduct of the air war. They have not understood why some seemingly irrational things have been done while other obviously vital things have not. Herein lies the problem and the reason for this report. In observing air warfare in the Third World, military analysts tend to make certain, often unconscious, assumptions about the logic behind the employment of airpower. These assumptions are based on our own historical experiences in four wars and are reinforced to a considerable degree by the successes of the Israeli Air Force against Arab air forces. Our institutional memory and perception holds that ours is a rational, sensible way to employ airpower to achieve military and national ends. Analysts tend to assume that any airpower practitioner will recognize the essential elements of a situation and will react in a "rational" manner, given his capabilities and limitations. They are not convinced that general rules for airpower employment are not essentially universal. But as one American analyst noted:

> We had a tendency to see the Israeli-Egyptian war as setting the pattern for future Third World conflicts. We discover today that Iraq and Iran are not Israel and Egypt, and that a war between countries like this can be much more chaotic and dangerous than we thought.[3]

This report attempts to make the Iran-Iraq air war a little less chaotic. It does not, however, present a day-by-day, blow-by-blow description of *what* happened in the air war. Rather it attempts to deduce the reasons *why* the air war progressed as it did. It shows how the combatants view the value of airpower, what aspects of airpower appear most important to Iranian and Iraqi national leaders, and how their values and needs led them to use airpower in ways quite apart from Western professional expectations.

This study has six parts. Chapter 1 discusses the role of airpower in prior Middle Eastern wars and concentrates on the lessons learned from these wars by the Arab states. Chapter 2 traces the development of the Iraqi and Iranian Air Forces in order to understand their historical and institutional bases in light of their actions against each other. Chapter 3 discusses the reasons for the war, while chapter 4 talks about the initial stage of conflict. Chapter 5 attempts to flesh out the question of why the air war went as it did in light of the comments in the preceding two chapters. The last chapter contains some conclusions on air operations between Iran and Iraq, and what Western observers may learn from them.

For convenience throughout this paper, the Iraqi Air Force is referred to as the IQAF and the Iranian Air Force as the IIAF—Imperial Iranian Air Force before the 1979 revolution, Islamic Iranian Air Force after it. While transliteration of Arabic and Persian personal and place names will not follow any single academic convention, it does follow a general guideline of being recognizable, familiar, pronounceable, and consistent.

## NOTES

1. Drew Middleton, "Iran-Iraq Impasse: Ground War Stalls, Yet Neither Side Exploits Air Power," *New York Times* (hereafter referred to as *NYT*), 6 October 1980, A14.

2. Harvey Sicherman, "Iraq and Iran at War: The Search for Security," *Orbis* 14 (Winter 1981): 713.

3. Geoffrey Kemp, quoted in Phillipe Rondot, "Iran-Iraq War Evaluated by French Journalist," Paris *Defense Nationale* in French, June 1981, 79–95, in *Joint Publications Research Service Near East/North African Report* (hereafter referred to as *JPRS*), no. 2357, 1 July 1981: 20.

# CHAPTER 1

# The Arab Air Warfare Experience

Both Iran and Iraq entered their war having a certain amount of historical experience in the use of tactical airpower. The IIAF had less actual combat experience having only fired in anger during periodic border problems with Iraq. More recently, however, they had used tactical airpower along with ground forces to assist the sultan of Oman in counterinsurgency operations in Dhofar, the western portion of Oman. In contrast, the IQAF had experienced combat operations during wars with Israel in 1948, 1967, and 1973. It had also operated extensively during the long running Kurdish insurgency that ended in 1975. And, of course, it had also engaged in periodic attacks along the Iranian border.

The Arabs, most notably the frontline states—Egypt, Syria, and Jordan—have had 30 years of lessons about airpower drilled into them by their experience against Israel. As this study will later show, some of these lessons also filtered into Iraqi and Iranian thinking. Many studies have been done on the Arab-Israeli wars, and the lessons about the use of airpower have been exhaustively argued—especially after the Six-Day War in 1967 and the October War in 1973. The great majority of these studies, however, discuss these lessons from the US or Israel perspective. Very few lay out the lessons absorbed by the losing side in these conflicts. While some lessons apply equally to both sides, it can be argued (and this study will do so) that the Arabs learned lessons that were, in some ways, quite different from those we learned. Legitimate arguments can be made that some of the lessons the Arabs have drawn are unrealistic and do not reflect rational thinking, at least from a Western perspective, but that is not the point. The point is that Arab military men perceive these things to be true insofar as they represent lessons they have learned; for them, their perception is their reality. Because the United States and the Arabs often read from totally different sheets of music, Americans sometimes misread Arab actions.[1]

While the rest of this chapter discusses air operations in the various Middle East conflicts from 1948 to 1973, it will not attempt to merely lay out the facts. Rather it will try to describe the wars from the Arab perspective so as to glean what lessons the Arabs—and, in some cases, the interested onlookers, the Iranians—took away from these encounters. The way things happened in the 1980-81 air war will make more sense if we have a sense of how the Arabs saw the results of their previous airpower efforts.

1

## The First Arab-Israeli War—1947-49

It is hard to say if the Arab air forces learned any airpower lessons from their experiences in the first war with Israel. Both sides were equipped with World War II surplus equipment, but neither had enough to do much more than isolated or harassing raids upon the other. Arab air forces at the outset of the war totaled three—Egypt, Iraq, and Syria. Royalist Egypt's air force, influenced by the British Royal Air Force (RAF), included about 40 Spitfires and utilized a few C-46s and C-47s as bombers.[2] Royalist Iraq, also RAF-influenced, had about 100 serviceable aircraft with Furies as the primary combat plane, some operating out of an advanced base in Transjordan.[3] The Syrians, French trained, had a few T-6 Harvards which could have been used as light bombers,[4] but they took little part in the air combat.[5]

During the first phase of the war, from November 1947—before the actual partition of Palestine—to summer 1948, just after the declaration of the new State of Israel, the Arabs had unchallenged air superiority. The fledgling Israeli Air Force (IAF) had no comparable aircraft with which to compete. Syria and Iraq were responsible for operations north of Tel Aviv, while Egypt was responsible for the area from Tel Aviv south.[6] Despite their unchallenged control of the air, the Arab air forces achieved no significant results. For example, almost daily Egyptian air raids on Tel Aviv were of nuisance value only, and Arab air forces were of almost no use to the disparate and disorganized Arab ground units. This was to continue throughout. Arab airpower was not an important factor and had little influence upon the ultimate outcome of any military operations.[7]

Things changed for the Arabs over the summer of 1948. The IAF, which started with 19 light auxiliary-type aircraft, got its first combat aircraft in May of that year. On the 29th, four Messerschmitts arrived from Czechoslovakia and more began to arrive daily. On 14 July, three B-17s which had been smuggled out of the United States arrived in Israel, having bombed Cairo en route. Soon they were making almost daily bombing runs on Arab positions. In August, the IAF received some P-51 Mustangs and Spitfires, further increasing their qualitative and now quantitative edge over the Arab air forces.[8] By the armistice, the IAF had 205 aircraft.[9] Additionally, throughout the year, Israel received foreign volunteers for its air force. In all, 700 volunteers arrived. Some were not Jewish, but most were World War II combat veterans and a number were fighter pilots with outstanding combat records.[10]

By September, the situation in the air had been reversed. In early summer, Arab flyers were still able to strafe Israeli positions with impunity. By late summer, however, the Iraqis had ceased operating in the north since they were unable to compete with the Messerschmitts by day and did not have any bombers for night operations. The Israelis, now possessing enough aircraft to begin to think about real airpower objectives, prepared in late fall to have the IAF support a ground offensive. IAF objectives were: (1) destroy the Arab air forces; (2) hit Arab tactical targets; (3) support Israeli ground forces; and (4) hit Arab strategic targets, notably Damascus and other smaller Arab towns. An October surprise attack on El 'Arīsh in the northern Sinai Peninsula caused a great deal of damage to Egyptian aircraft caught on the ground and appeared to demoralize totally the Egyptian Air Force (EAF). For the rest of the war, the EAF hardly ever challenged Israeli control of the air.[11]

## Lessons—1948

It is hard to detect that the Arab states derived any lessons about airpower utilization from their first experience with the Israelis. Arab confusion and bickering after the war reflected their performance during the war. For the Arabs, the most significant result of the war was political—the subsequent radicalization of Arab politics. Searching for the reasons for the loss of Arab Palestine, many fixed the blame on Arab leaders. The prime minister of Iraq was forced to resign, the emir of Transjordan was assassinated, the Syrian government began its sorry succession of military coups, and the royal dynasty in Egypt was ousted by army officers. But the most salient fact concerning airpower from the Arab viewpoint was that airpower, in their hands, was not very effective in achieving their military goals while Israeli control of the air in the later stages of the war was not the decisive cause for their defeat. The Arabs showed no sign they felt the air force could be a decisive military weapon. They seemed inclined to consider it useful mostly as a defensive weapon. Consequently, Arab offensive sorties were not much more than harassment missions. One lesson that was absorbed, however, was defensively oriented. They had learned there was a need to be able to control the air over their troops in the relatively coverless Middle Eastern topography. They could see that the army, the most important element of their military structure, could be demoralized, if not necessarily defeated by aerial bombardment. Egyptian troops—including future President Gamal Abdel Nasser—surrounded in the Falluja pocket in southern Israel were bombed almost daily by Israeli B-17s. Despite the severe hardships the troops experienced from the bombings, the Egyptians held out until the armistice.[12]

Despite their overtly offensive aims in the 1948 war—destruction of the Jewish state in Palestine—the Arabs did not seem to see the offensive potential in their air forces. They did not seek out the enemy air force and they quit the area of combat when the enemy air force challenged them. They could see a defensive role for the air forces, protecting their own troops from bombardment, but they still did not see bombardment as decisive. They had yet to experience, however, the effects of unopposed bombardment on troops forced to retreat long distances over the desert. That lesson was yet to come.

## The Suez War—29 October–7 November 1956

One of the results of the 1948 war was, as previously noted, the overthrow of the Egyptian monarchy. The Free Officers, a group of military men led by Lt Col Gamal

3

Abdel Nasser, forced King Farouk to abdicate on 23 July 1952 which, in turn, led to the formal declaration of Egypt as a republic a year later. As leader of republican Egypt, the charismatic Nasser very quickly irritated Western leaders as he loudly denounced Western influence in the Middle East while simultaneously advocating the overthrow of conservative, pro-West Arab governments. He especially embittered the British by his vehement hostility to the British-sponsored Baghdad Pact (a posture that kept Jordan and Syria from joining) and by his strident denunciations of British control over the Suez Canal—a condition that had existed since 1882. He also deeply antagonized France, then sulking over the recent loss of its Indochina colonies, by his overt support of Algerian rebels seeking the end of French rule in that country. His support was both moral in the form of strident rhetoric and physical in the providing of arms for the rebels. Atop all this was the continued mutual hostility between Egypt and Israel. While much of Nasser's anti-Israeli rhetoric was designed primarily to secure Egyptian leadership of an Arab world where verbal overbidding is necessary for political success, Israel prudently noted several actual manifestations of malevolence, such as Egypt's refusal to allow Israeli shipping through the Suez Canal and its closure of the Strait of Tiran—two actions that damaged the Israeli economy. Moreover, the 1955 arms deal with Czechoslovakia, which would gain Egypt 86 MiG-15s and 39 Il-28s as well as tanks, guns, antiaircraft artillery (AAA), and other weapons, was a situation that Tel Aviv viewed as a direct, if future-oriented, threat to the safety of the Jewish state.[13] Thus by 1956, three states had reasons to wish the end of Colonel Nasser and they jointly planned to see it happen.

Israel had in 1955 begun planning an operation, later named Operation Kadesh, to seize control of the Strait of Tiran. By July 1956, the Israeli government had decided that the state of Israeli-Arab relations was intolerable and gave tentative approval for war. Coincidental in timing, but unrelated to Israeli planning, Great Britain had decided that it too would use military force in Egypt. The final straw for London was Egypt's 26 July 1956 nationalization of the Suez Canal. In early August, British Prime Minister Robert Anthony Eden decided to use force to restore the canal to its "rightful owners," the (British) Suez Canal Corporation. France—for its own aforementioned reasons—joined Britain, and planning for a joint military operation began. In October, Israel was invited to join in the assault.[14] The final plan envisaged an Israeli attack into the Sinai, ostensibly as retaliation for fedayeen guerrilla raids, followed by an Anglo-French ultimatum that both sides disengage, each moving to a line 10 miles east and west of the canal while British and French troops occupied the canal to "protect" it. If Nasser refused the ultimatum, they would force their way in.[15] The Anglo-French operation was called Musketeer.

From the beginning, elimination or neutralization of the EAF was a first priority for both Musketeer and Kadesh planners. While Israel felt it could probably handle the EAF had Israel gone alone on Operation Kadesh, it would not join in the Anglo-French assault unless Israel proper was protected from Egyptian retaliatory bombing.[16] As French Gen André Beaufre put it, Israel wanted the surest form of air cover—the destruction of the EAF on the ground.[17] Neutralization of the EAF was also a prerequisite for the Anglo-French invasion forces.

The air force the three allies were so concerned about totaled fewer than 300 aircraft (including 45 MiG-15s, 40 Vampires, 38 Meteors, 8 Furies, 49 Il-28s, 20 C-46s, and 20 C-47s); however, only about 130 planes (60 fighters, 10 Il-28s, and 60 transports) were actually operational.[18] The EAF had too few pilots and those they did have were of poor quality; most of them were incapable of efficiently using the recently arrived Soviet equipment. The number of aircraft the EAF was able to put into the air was much lower than anyone had estimated.[19]

To deal with this air force, the allies had at their disposal 200 Royal Navy fighters off three carriers, 50 French Navy fighters off two carriers, nine squadrons of RAF bombers (120 aircraft in all), four squadrons of RAF fighter-bombers (100 aircraft), and four French fighter-bomber wings (77 F-84s and 25 Mystère IVs). The IAF had 155 more aircraft (including 9 Mystères, 25 Ouragans, 25 Meteors, 29 P-51s, 16 Mosquitos, 20 T-6 Harvards, 16 C-47s, and 2 B-17s).[20] The IAF was to assist the Kadesh forces while the French and British were to destroy the EAF. The revised Musketeer plan envisaged three phases for the Suez operation. Phase one was a 36-hour destruction of the EAF. Phase two was a 10-14 day, round-the-clock air offensive to disrupt the Egyptian economy, communications and transportation network, and army along with a psychological campaign to cripple Egyptian civilian morale—the "aero-psychological campaign." Phase three was the occupation of the canal area.[21]

The Israeli invasion began in the afternoon of 29 October. Britain and France delivered their ultimatum to Cairo and to Tel Aviv as part of the plan to appear as an honest broker on 30 October. When Nasser, as anticipated, rejected it, Musketeer began. At 1900 hours, 31 October, RAF Canberras and Valiants, operating at high altitude and using flares for illumination, dropped both contact and delayed-action bombs on four Egyptian airfields. As Egypt had no early warning system, the RAF encountered no EAF opposition. The night attack with small payloads, however, was not markedly successful in destroying the EAF. Early morning reconnaissance on 1 November showed potted runways and fires, but few damaged planes. The EAF, in fact, had managed to save some airframes. Russian and Czech pilots flew some Il-28s and MiG-15s to Saudi and Syrian safe havens. Twenty more Il-28s were flown south to Luxor. But allied air forces soon finished up the EAF. Later on the same day, French and British aircraft, operating from both Cyprus and off the carriers, made low-level passes on EAF planes at 12 airfields, using mostly rockets and cannons. By the end of the day, very accurate gunnery had destroyed 260 or so Egyptian planes on the ground at a cost of 7 allied planes lost to moderate antiaircraft fire or accident. Of the 49 Il-28s that caused so much concern to Israel, only the 20 at Luxor remained (and those too were destroyed on the 2d by French F-84s operating out of Israel). Though the EAF was to fly a few sorties every day for the rest of the war, its isolated strafing runs could not alter the outcome of the ground fighting. Within the first 24 hours of the war, the EAF had been destroyed as a fighting force.[22]

The air portion of Egypt's war was essentially over before it began. For the rest of the war, Musketeer aircraft concentrated on strafing other Egyptian military targets while the Israeli Air Force freely struck at Egyptian army units which had been ordered to retreat to the canal to avoid being cut off in the Sinai.

## Lessons—1956

Whether the EAF, or other regional observers, learned any lessons from the 1956 experience is again an open question. For the majority of the Egyptian populace and the Arab world, the memory of the crushing military defeat was erased by the euphoria over Egypt's political victory. Under United States pressure, France and Great Britain were forced to leave the Suez Canal and to concede its sovereignty to Egypt; and Israel was forced to return to the 1949 armistice borders, returning the Sinai to Egypt. Some facets of the air operations, however, must have been noted.

Unlike 1948, Egypt in 1956 possessed enough airframes to pose a potentially effective threat to would-be enemies. Yet, that potential was eliminated by enemy airpower utilizing the principle of surprise to destroy the EAF on the ground. At one swoop, the enemy had ensured their air supremacy, thus leaving Egypt and its armies almost without defenses from air attack. Enemy aircraft, attacking first, completely took the employment initiative away from the EAF, forcing it into a reactive mode (and an extremely limited mode at that). Even though the French and British destroyed the EAF, Israel obviously realized that airpower used in a first strike, offensive mode was the way to defend its homeland from attack or its troops from interference from the air. But there was no sign Egyptian airmen viewed airpower in the same offensive light. Allied airpower first attacked Egyptian air assets. On the other hand, Egyptian aircraft, wherever they operated, acted to defend airspace or to defend their own soldiers by striking at enemy troops.[23] No allied aircraft were attacked at their home bases.

Another fact that had to be noted was the vulnerability of aircraft on the ground. Most of the EAF's losses were to strafing or rocket fire. The desirability of revetments or hardened shelters was obvious. The EAF did have one answer for vulnerability of their planes on the ground; they flew them out to safe havens beyond the battle area (though Luxor later turned out not to be so safe).

But the poor EAF response to these lessons, further developed in the next section, was to hurt them in 1967. They had clear warning. Moshe Dayan published his diary in Hebrew in 1965 and in English in 1966. In it he stated that the EAF must be destroyed on the ground for an Israeli invasion to succeed.[24]

In reviewing the events of late 1956, one lesson that had to penetrate into Egyptian thinking was the recognition that troops in the desert, without some sort of air defense, are highly vulnerable to air attack. Israel's answer to this situation was offensive counterair—destroy enemy air on the ground or in the air before it could attack Israeli ground forces. Egypt did not yet seem to have a comparable answer. It patently did not have an offensive counterair idea. Any offensive ideas it seemed to have were limited to interdiction and deep attacks on the enemy homeland rather than against specific enemy air assets. The fact that Egypt regained the Sinai without a fight and rapidly rebuilt its air force with Soviet aid allowed the Egyptians to defer facing up to the inadequacies of their thinking as well as the total realities of their situation.[25]

No other Arab states got into the 1956 war. This meant that any lessons the Iraqi and Iranian Air Forces might have learned were limited. Royalist Iraq was in the last years of its life as the pressures were building that would lead to the violent and bitter 1958 revolution. But in 1956, Iraq was allied with Britain in the Baghdad Pact and the bulk of the IQAF was composed of British-supplied Vampire and Venom fighters. Iraq, like Britain, was in an anomalous situation with regards to Israel. Iraq moved troops to Jordan to help that state fend off potential Israeli attacks. Should Israel have hit at Jordan as well as Egypt, Britain would have to sort out its alliances before proceeding since England would have been Israel's ally in the Sinai but her enemy on the Jordanian border.[26]

In Iran, the IIAF was still in a formative stage. The shah was still working to consolidate his control in the aftermath of the 1951-53 Mohammed Mossadegh era. Development of his military as a bulwark of his throne was a high-priority task for the shah. But the IIAF in 1956 was just beginning to receive its first combat aircraft, 75 F-84s that would arrive from 1956 to 1958.[27]

## The Six-Day War—1967

Eleven years later, the Arab air forces, especially the Egyptian, had not adequately reacted to the lessons of 1956. A partial reason was that the EAF was still living in a fool's paradise—thinking defensively, planning for retaliation, and expecting that it could pick the time and place for combat. To a large extent, the EAF's posture was a reflection of Nasser's own feeling about the situation. Egypt's defensive orientation was noted in 1956 when, despite its verbal hostility to Israel and the West, it felt itself the innocent, assaulted by external enemies. The year 1967 was much the same. Israel may well have decided to act in reaction to Arab threats because it could not risk that they might actually try to carry them out. But for all his bombast, Nasser clearly did not anticipate launching an attack. In the Arab game of verbal one-upmanship, Nasser went, in May 1967, beyond his previously stated objective of *deterring* Israeli aggression to state his intention of settling the Palestinian question (by force, implicitly). Yet he was clearly thinking he could pull off another 1956 and gain his ends through political, not military, means. He clearly expected that if war came, Egypt would not start it. He did say on 27 May, "The battle against Israel will be a general one, and our basic objective will be to destroy Israel." Yet he preceded that statement with, "If Israel embarks on an aggression against Syria or Egypt, the battle. . . ." This commitment to a second strike posture was explicitly stated on a number of occasions just prior to the war.[28] The EAF had to be conditioned to a certain extent by this attitude. The EAF knew it was not going to launch a war nor did it fully appreciate or respect its enemy. The EAF told itself its 1956 defeat was caused by Britain and France. In 1967, the EAF still did not respect IAF capabilities. It had not dispersed, it had not hardened its airfields, and it had not placed its aircraft out of Israeli reach.[29] Conditioned to a state of belligerency without war, committed to a retaliatory posture, the EAF continued business as usual as May turned into June.

The military situation in the Six-Day War can be concisely stated—led by its air force, the Israelis crushed the Arabs. Some of the important reasons for the IAF success were: (1) maximum surprise allowed the IAF to hit the bulk of Arab aircraft while they were still on the ground, (2) excellent target intelligence which both located Arab aircraft and identified the most advantageous time to strike them, (3) low-level attack runs for accuracy (shades of 1956), and (4) the IAF's rapid aircraft turnaround capability. The EAF was wiped out again; according to the 1973 EAF commander, Hosni Mubarak, the EAF lost over 90 percent of its aircraft in the first day or so and, even more important, most of its meager supply of pilots.[30] As the Egyptian Air Force was being destroyed on the morning of 5 June, the other Arab air forces attempted some small, half-hearted, and poorly coordinated retaliatory raids on Israel. They caused minimal damage, but Israel's return strikes did not. The Royal Jordanian Air Force was eliminated on the ground during turnarounds. The Syrian Air Force was next taken out and lastly the Iraqi Air Force was damaged by a strike at H-3 airfield, the closest Iraqi airfield to Israel.[31] The Royal Saudi Air Force was not hit. The Saudis apparently learned early what was happening to the EAF, recognized the futility of the situation, and elected not to enter into a hopeless encounter with the IAF.[32] In all, the IAF struck 25 of 26 Arab air bases on 5 June, effectively eliminating the Arab air forces and freeing Israeli ground forces from air attacks.[33]

Without air cover, Arab armies were again easy target for Israeli air. The Egyptian commander in chief made the same decision on 6 June 1967 as he had made in 1956; he ordered the Egyptian army to withdraw from the Sinai to behind the Suez Canal.[34] Egyptian soldiers in 1967 suffered the same fate they had in 1956, only worse. Israeli air, generally unopposed by the EAF, wrecked the disorganized Egyptian columns moving west. On the other front, Israeli air was even more important. The Jordanian army on the West Bank fought well, but without air defense, its columns were smashed and its positions were pummeled. When Israeli ground forces found themselves in a tight spot, they could call on air support to bail them out; the Jordanians could not. The situation was much the same for Syrian forces on the Golan Heights. Despite undeniable heroics by Israeli army men, there is serious doubt whether or not the Syrians could have been dislodged without heavy Israeli air attacks. The IAF flew more ground attack sorties against Syrian forces in the Golan Heights than against all

8

other Arab forces combined.[35] The IAF contribution to the total Israeli effort was vital. Trevor Dupuy noted:

> With almost complete control of the air the Israelis were able to capitalize on the ground on their initial advantage of surprise and their superior combat effectiveness without having to defend against air attacks from their enemies' air weapons. The full significance of this air superiority, and the devastating effect of the air attacks upon the Arab ground troops, seems not to have been fully appreciated even by the Israelis, who after all have never been under truly effective hostile air attack themselves.[36]

The defeat was a shattering experience for all Arabs. Despite efforts to explain it away, or refer to it as only a "setback,"[37] the reality of defeat hit hard. Whereas the 1948 and 1956 losses had, in the main, affected only small portions of the Arab nation—military officers, for example—the 1967 defeat affected all Arabs. Moreover, "the emotional and political impact of this crushing defeat was enormous since it struck at the very heart of Arab values and Arab self-image."[38] Israel played on this factor by successfully publicizing the war as a test between the Jewish David and the Arab Goliath, both to gain Western support for Israel and to cause Israel's enemies to question themselves. The impact was enough to jolt Muslim Arabs into a soul-searching introversion to find a reason for the defeat. In many ways, 1967 marked the beginning of the most recent Muslim revival period as many Muslims, unwilling or incapable of accepting Israeli military and organizational superiority, saw the defeat as God's retribution for their having strayed from the proper Islamic path.[39]

But many Arabs, in their reaction to defeat, found psychic refuge in refusing to admit it had happened. King Hussein said, "We are not defeated. A defeated man is one whose morale has been broken. Our morale has not been weakened."[40] An Arab summit two months after the war outlined the principles of Arab relations with victorious Israel—no war, no peace, no recognition or negotiations with Israel. The losers of the war refused to admit their conqueror existed.

## Lessons—1967

But Arab leaders did, of course, recognize that they had been humiliated and they began to face up to the task of analyzing the reasons. The most important lesson was that Israeli strength was real, and the Arabs could not trifle with Israel; if Arab lands and honor were to be regained, they would have to be regained with blood. Postwar Egyptian analyses decided that the Arab military defeat was caused by a general misconduct of operations, the lack of sufficient Arab planning and coordination, the effect of Israel's surprise air attack, and poor intelligence estimates.[41]

Egypt, especially, undertook to rectify its miserable conduct of military operations by creating a new army made up of new Arabs. The old leaders were removed—Commander in Chief Amer was jailed when he supposedly tried a coup, and Air Force Chief General Mahmoud and a number of officers were tried and jailed for misconduct. By 1969, the EAF had been purged and reorganized three times due to Nasser's dissatisfaction with its performance.[42] Within the army, key leaders were identified and given the authority to make changes. Higher quality personnel were drafted as officers; and the training was toughened, made realistic, and repeated enough so that the men would have faith in their leaders, their arms, and themselves. Most important, the men were not training to maintain static positions as they had in the past. They trained knowing that a war with Israel was inevitable and that they would carry the brunt of it.[43] To a lesser degree, the Syrian army did the same.

To this end, planning and coordination were improved. An Egyptian war planning staff was selected and charged with devising a plan that took into account the real strengths and limitations of both the Israelis and the Arabs, one which would lead to a restitution of Arab honor and, hopefully, victory. Egyptian officers took the lead, but coordination with Syria was maintained and facilitated by the leaders of the two states. To preserve secrecy, all other Arab states were left uninformed.[44]

All three frontline Arab states—Egypt, Syria, and Jordan—recognized Israel's ability to win total control of the air at the outset of any hostilities. This meant Arab armies would have to face Israel's combined air-ground team with no help from their own air. As previously noted, air was a major reason for Israeli success on the Syrian and Jordanian fronts in 1967. The EAF saw that its failure to appreciate the damage the French and British had done to its unprotected aircraft in 1956 had led the EAF to suffer the same fate at Israel's hand in 1967. Therefore, an extensive program to disperse their aircraft and harden their shelters was begun.[45]

At first, however, the EAF was so totally preoccupied with the idea of preventing a repeat of Israel's 1967 preemptive strike that all its thoughts were concentrated on how to neutralize the IAF by gaining air superiority.[46] But the Egyptians gradually came to recognize that Arab air forces were years behind the IAF in capability and were unlikely to catch up in the foreseeable future. This is the fourth aspect of their 1967 lesson—they realistically looked at themselves, admitted their shortcomings, and began to plan on the basis of realistic estimates concerning their own and their enemy's capabilities. For Egypt, this led to two lessons. First, the EAF would not be used beyond its capabilities, it would not challenge the IAF, and it would be used mostly for defense. Second, since the EAF could not compete, achievement of air superiority was unattainable. But the ground forces needed protection from Israeli air. The Arab answer was to seek local air control instead of air superiority, to seek to control the air over their forces using a dense air defense net rather than to throw their air force away in a hopeless attempt to destroy the IAF.

Gen Saad Shazly, Egypt's chief of staff in the 1973 war, listed his reasons for needing an air force. They were to provide, in this order: (1) air cover, (2) close air support, (3) reconnaissance, and (4) interdiction or deep strike.[47] He felt that the EAF's weakness was so fundamental that it should not be brought into direct conflict with the IAF if at all possible. The EAF was to be used in a calculated and cautious manner. Ground attack missions were to be hit-and-run affairs where Israeli air cover was unlikely. Chance air-to-air encounters were to be avoided.[48] When Israeli aircraft approached Egyptian rear areas, EAF fighters were to be scrambled but only to patrol designated areas. Air-to-air engagements outside these areas were not permitted unless part of a preapproved plan. No engagements were to be accepted at unfavorable odds.[49] Gen Abdul Moneim Riyadh, Egypt's commander in chief from 1967 to 1969, stated there could be no battle with Israel without air defense and acceptable air assistance. He did not mention air superiority.[50] His successor (after his death) as commander in chief, Gen Ahmed Ismail decided that while the army had to fight, it could not depend upon the air force for its life. Thus, the EAF was to be used for ground support where required but would not be squandered in combat with the IAF. The EAF would not be tasked with winning air superiority over the Sinai.[51] The Egyptian Air Defense Command was thus organized as a separate service in 1968, and it was to have the role of giving the army a measure of protection.[52] These lessons were borne out in the War of Attrition (1969–70). Egyptian (and Soviet) attempts to compete with the IAF in air-to-air combat resulted in nothing but losses.[53]

Thus, the Arabs reversed the commonly accepted role of airpower. While Israel was quite certain the Arabs would have to try to gain air superiority in order to make a successful ground assault, Egypt and Syria decided that their armies would move under an air defense umbrella that would hopefully inflict enough damage on the IAF that it would either be forced to refrain from attacking them or be forced out of optimum attack envelopes. Knowing they could not duplicate Israel's 1967 feat, their plans maximized their advantages and minimized the IAF's. Their ground forces would remain inside their air defense umbrella. Their air forces would be preserved as a strategic reserve to impose caution on the enemy, to step into possible breaches of their air defense system, or to exploit the situation after the air defense system weakened the enemy air force.[54]

Having placed their air forces firmly behind their armies, Egypt and Syria were ready militarily in 1973. But the Egyptians had one more item in their arsenal, an item which Iraq would lack in 1980–81 and which would lead Baghdad into a morass. Egypt had a well-thought-out political strategy which directed its military strategy. In its war with Iran, Iraq's political, and hence its military, strategy was not so well thought out.

The Egyptian leadership, in conscious or innate understanding of Clausewitz, had political goals and strategies for which their military strategies were expressly tailored. Mohamed Heikal noted in *The Road to Ramadan* that it was a vital necessity in a limited war to have a political strategy ready to take over when the fighting ceases. Their political strategy would direct the military phase of the conflict and would also direct the negotiating phase which was to follow. It was as vital to have a strategy for conflict termination as it was to have one for conflict initiation.[55] The Egyptian leadership knew Israel did not respect them militarily, and the rest of the world likewise did not take them seriously. Therefore, the Egyptians reasoned that Israel

11

must be shocked into the recognition that the Arabs must be dealt with as more or less equals. This meant war and it had to be a successful war. Success for Egypt did not mean objective military victory; it meant some recognizable gain and, above all, no crushing defeat. Since so little was expected of them, any success would be viewed as a great national triumph. Second, a solution to their problem with Israel was not possible without intervention by the superpowers who would not intervene unless the situation threatened them. This meant a continuation of a "no peace, no war" status quo would not do. Thus, it had to be war in which superpower interests were threatened, if only by threatening them through risking their reputations by the performance of their arms as used by the actual combatants.

So it was to be war in 1973. But, on this occasion, Israel for the first time was forced to react to Arab strategic initiative rather than the other way around. For Egypt, any gain meant victory since Egyptian leaders knew if the war was violent enough to bring superpower intervention, neither superpower would allow its client to lose. With lessons born of their crushing defeats, the Arabs developed an airpower doctrine accurately reflecting their abilities. Arab airpower was to support their armies and their armies were to regain Arab dignity.

# The October War—1973

The war to restore Arab dignity began on 6 October 1973 with Egyptian airstrikes on Israeli positions in the Sinai. The October War thus began in much the same manner as had the 1956 and 1967 wars—with a surprise air attack. But there were to be two startling differences. First, in 1973, the Arab side took the initiative, forcing Israel to react to it rather than the other way around. Second, the airstrikes were not designed as a way to attain air superiority as had been the case in 1956 and 1967. Instead, their attacks were carried out as the leading edge of the main thrust which was to be an infantry attack. Air superiority was not the goal of the attacks nor was it necessary for success in the overall concept of operations for the attackers.

The Egyptian attack was the opening salvo in a war they planned to be limited, both in scope and duration.[56] The Egyptian planning staff had developed their concept in full recognition of Israeli strengths. Commander in Chief Ismail listed them as: air superiority (note that he concedes this to the IAF at the start), technological skill, efficient training, and reliance on quick aid from the United States. Israeli disadvantages in Ismail's view were: long lines of communication, limited manpower that could not accept heavy losses, an economy that could not afford a long war, and the "wanton evil of conceit" (to Ismail, the refusal to respect its enemies).[57]

Conceding, as they did, the fact that the IAF would have air superiority, the opening EAF airstrike was to be a hit-and-run operation. The Egyptians felt they had no chance of achieving a repetition of Israel's success in 1967. The IAF was always on alert with its aircraft dispersed on many airfields. Israel also had a very capable air defense system. Finally, most of the IAF was beyond Egyptian reach due to the short range of most of Egypt's Soviet-built fighters.[58] The Arab attack would live or die, not with air superiority but with a measure of air control which was to be gained by ground-based air defense. The army was to be kept under this air defense umbrella while the air force was to be used mainly for air defense support, engaging the IAF only where ground-based air defense was unavailable.[59] According to Maj Gen D. K. Palit, an Indian observer sympathetic to the Arab side, the Arab high commands (here Egyptian and Syrian), recognizing the need to restrict their air operations in the face of Israeli superiority, apparently had a concept of air operations designed to gain the following objectives: (1) to make an opening, surprise attack on Israeli forward positions, radar sites, and communications installations in support of the army assault; (2) to compel the IAF to spread its efforts over two sectors and on as broad a front as possible within each sector, thus reducing its ability to inflict damage; (3) to utilize air as part of the overall air defense, air control philosophy; and (4) to support ground operations, but staying within their own air defense umbrella except in emergencies.[60]

The results of the implementation of this philosophy were mixed. According to Palit, the pre-H-hour airstrikes in the Sinai were believed to be effective.[61] Twelve or more targets were hit—gun concentrations, command and control communications nodes, radar sites, airfields, and Hawk batteries—with enough success that the planned second strike was called off.[62] Conversely, Israeli Army General Adan later wrote he was surprised at how *in*effective the Egyptian strikes were. He implied the reason the planned second wave did not materialize was that the IAF had shot down 68 out of the 190 to 240 (depending on whose account you believe) attackers.[63] The truth is probably somewhere in between—the attacks were not expected to be crushing, rather they were only to delay Israeli responses. Thus, Egyptian planners, who did not want to expose their air forces to the IAF any more than necessary, could well have concluded that the first wave had done sufficient damage and resulted in enough losses.

But the key fact for the Arab side in the 1973 air war was not their mediocre offensive showing, but their defensive. Much has been written since 1973 on the supposed lessons of the war concerning the strengths and limitations of the offense versus the defense. A variant of this theme—the aircraft versus missile debate—continues today without a clear winner. But for the Arabs, one fact is incontrovertible—their concept of air control through heavy use of surface-to-air missiles (SAMs) caused severe IAF losses and forced the IAF to change its fighting style. On the Suez front, the air defense barrier proved very effective. In the course of the first afternoon, at least 10 IAF planes were downed. In this high-threat environment, the IAF aircraft found themselves forced either to higher-than-optimum altitudes for ground support or out of the area entirely.[64] On the Golan front the IAF also fared poorly, losing even more aircraft to Syrian air defense forces on the first day.[65] During Israeli counterattacks on the Suez front on 8–10 October, the IAF was held at bay by Egyptian air defense while Israeli tanks took a beating.[66] General Adan noted that it was not until 12 October that the skies were safe enough for the IAF that

13

he could allocate aircraft to his brigades in a continuous manner.[67] Probably the most important fact for the Arab side was that they were not routed, and Israeli aircraft did not have free rein to shoot up retreating Arab columns as they had in the two previous wars. But they also realized how helpless their armies could be whenever they had to face the IAF outside their air defense umbrella. Whenever Egyptian or Syrian forces got outside their umbrella, the IAF destroyed them.[68] Shazly stated it pithily: "The decisiveness of the encounter was a reminder, if we needed one, of how open our ground forces were to air attack the moment they left our SAM umbrella."[69]

Arab euphoria at not being routed and causing severe IAF losses notwithstanding, their air control through air defense concept only kept them from being defeated, it did not bring them to victory.[*] Pakistani Gen S. A. el-Edroos succinctly summed up the Arab air forces' dilemma. To him, the October War illustrated the inherent offensive capability of an air force and the potential defensive capability of an effective air defense system. But the Arabs only used one-half the equation, they relied on their air defense as a Maginot Line in the sky. The inevitable result was that when the air defense systems were breached by a combination of Israeli ground and air forces, the IAF mauled the Arab air forces. To el-Edroos, the severely restricted strategic and tactical roles assigned to the Arab air forces were faulty in that they placed an essentially offensive arm into a defensive "straitjacket" with negative results all around.[70] In fact, the Arab response—once the air defense wall was breached—was ineffective. Arab airmen were aggressive; but once forced to operate outside their narrowly restricted defensive role, they suffered greatly. Palit noted the suicidal efforts of the Syrian Air Force to salvage what they could on the Golan Heights.[71] Most of the EAF sorties were flown, and most of its losses were suffered, in the final days of the war when the umbrella had been breached. Brave as they were, Egyptian pilots suffered their losses without materially affecting the situation in the air or on the ground.[72]

But despite this, the Arab perception of success remained unshaken. They concluded that ground-based missiles can stop both tanks and aircraft.[73] More important for the Arab psyche, however, was their ability to hold their own against an Israeli force that had advertised itself and was generally perceived as invincible.

## Lessons—1973

So, what lessons did they draw from the war? First, as previously described, they felt they had pioneered a concept of air control in which the weaker party would use ground-based air defense to support an offensive while holding their air forces back as a strategic reserve. Second, this air control concept depended on tremendous amounts of SAMs—as they fired them in salvos in order to get as high a probability

---

[*]Of course, this is all mere argumentation anyway. Israel, from our perspective, clearly won the military battles, but the Arabs say they planned only not to lose and thus won the political war. There is something to this argument, as the Israeli settlers who recently had to leave the Sinai can attest.

of kill as they could. The supply factor in turn depends on superpower connections. It would have been more difficult for Syria and Egypt to have launched their attack had they not felt reasonably sure they could receive resupply of their critical needs, which were going to be SAMs. Just as they had with the overall strategic issue, the Arab side—in addressing the resupply issue—had firmly tied political realities with military strategies. They knew that the Soviet Union could not afford to let them lose badly; hence, they would be resupplied. And, if Soviet arms appeared to be performing well, they knew the Soviet Union would want to ensure that fact be well known to the world and would want to resupply them. So the second lesson was that military objectives must be closely coordinated with political realities in order to achieve success. Such realities, however, may be obvious only to the Arab decisionmaking elite where decisions may well reflect their perceptions more than they do objective reality.

## Wrap-up—The Arab Wars

Even though they achieved a measure of success in 1973, the 1967 war was still the most important war for the Arab countries. They found reasons in 1948 and 1956 to explain away their losses, but the 1967 defeat was so stark that they, for the first time, really had to examine themselves.

In large measure, it was the Egyptians who did the best job. Unlike Syria and Iraq, which have been beset with chronic coups, Egypt has had relative stability at the top since 1952. Thus a professional officer corps has developed more in Egypt than in the other two countries. Jordan has a very professional officer corps too, but it is so poor in both fiscal and manpower resources that it cannot be a major player.

Planning for 1973, the Egyptians were able to assess forthrightly their weaknesses and to devise a plan that could camouflage them even as it hit hard at enemy vulnerabilities. Syrian planners were a poor second cousin to the Egyptians in this effort, and the Iraqis were completely out of the picture. The problem for the Syrians and Iraqis is that they may have learned the lessons of 1973 only partly. Syria, which gained little but self-respect in 1973, was slower than Egypt to agree to a cease-fire. Iraq, which gained nothing other than casualties, refused to agree to a cease-fire and, in a show of pique, withdrew its forces from the confrontation lines. There is reason to believe that the combination of less than totally professional military leadership at the top (a phenomenon of endemic political instability) and a slightly unrealistic appreciation of their abilities could have left both Syria and Iraq more in a pre-1967 mode of thinking than in a pre-1973. They think they won in 1973, but they may well have not looked too closely at what that war "won" for them.

# NOTES

1. For an expanded discussion of this situation see John W. Amos II. *Arab-Israeli Military/Political Relations: Arab Perceptions and the Politics of Escalation* (New York: Pergamon Press. 1979). 4.

2. Netanel Lorch. *The Edge of the Sword: Israel's War of Independence. 1947–1949* (New York: G. P. Putnam's Sons. 1961). 225.

3. Edgar O'Ballance. *The Arab-Israeli War. 1948* (London: Faber and Faber. Ltd.. 1956). 82.

4. Lorch. 225.

5. "Arab Air Power. Part Four." *Air International* 13 (September 1977): 149.

6. Lorch. 228.

7. O'Ballance. *Arab-Israeli War. 1948.* 123.

8. Lorch. 230. 315. 362.

9. Zeev Schiff. "The Israeli Air Force." *Air Force Magazine* 59. no. 8 (August 1976): 32.

10. Lorch. 317. 364.

11. Ibid.. 362. 364.

12. Ibid.. 434.

13. Col Trevor N. Dupuy (US Army Ret.). *Elusive Victory: The Arab-Israeli Wars. 1947–1974* (New York: Harper & Row. Publishers. Inc.. 1978). 132-34; and SIPRI (Stockholm International Peace Research Institute). *The Arms Trade with the Third World* (New York: Humanities Press. 1971). 520. 838-39

14. Dupuy. 136–43.

15. Anthony Nutting. *No End of a Lesson: The Story of Suez* (New York: Clarkson N. Potter. Inc.. 1967). 115-16.

16. Ibid.. 80. 102.

17. André Beaufre. *The Suez Expedition 1956.* translated by Richard Barry (New York: Frederick A. Praeger. Inc.. 1969). 67.

18. Dupuy. 212.

19. Roy Fullick and Geoffrey Powell. *Suez: The Double War* (London: Hamish Hamilton. 1979). 91.

20. Dupuy. 212–14.

21. Kennett Love. *Suez: The Twice-Fought War* (New York: McGraw-Hill. 1969). 458.

22. Love. 526–28; Nutting. 126–27; Fulick and Powell. 109–14. 120-21; Robert Henriques. *A Hundred Hours to Suez: An Account of Israel's Campaign in the Sinai Peninsula* (New York: Viking Press. 1957). 153.

23. Love. 508–9; Henriques. 153.

24. Love. 443.

25. SIPRI. 522.

26. Nutting. 84–87.

27. SIPRI. 840.

28. Amos. 57–62.

29. Jon D. Glassman. *Arms for the Arabs: The Soviet Union and War in the Middle East* (Baltimore: Johns Hopkins University Press. 1975). 45.

30. Amos. 294.

31. Dupuy. 247; Stefan Geisenheyner. "The Arab Air Forces: Will They Try Again?" *Air Force Magazine* 51 (July 1968): 47–48.

32. Amos. 296.

33. Dupuy. 247.

34. Ibid.. 267.

35. Ibid.. 295–96. 311; Edgar O'Ballance. *The Third Arab-Israeli War* (Hamden. Conn.: Archon Books. 1972). 216–20. 257; Amos. 67–68.

36. Dupuy. 335.

37. Amos, 69.

38. Ibid., 69.

39. Ibid., 75-80; and Martin S. Kramer, *Political Islam*, in Georgetown University Center for Strategic and International Studies, *The Washington Papers*, vol. 8, no. 73 (Beverly Hills: Sage Publications, 1980): 18.

40. Amos, 69-70.

41. Ibid., 81.

42. Ibid.

43. Hassan el-Badri, Taha el-Magdoub, and Mohammed Dia el-Din Zohdy, *The Ramadan War, 1973* (Dunn Loring, Va.: T. N. Dupuy Assocs., Inc., 1978), 40-41.

44. Maj Gen D. K. Palit, *Return to Sinai: The Arab Offensive October 1973* (Dehra Dun and New Delhi: Palit and Palit Publishers, 1974), 75-76.

45. Amos, 81; Geisenheyner, 47; Mohamed Heikal, *The Road to Ramadan* (New York: Ballantine Books, 1976), 45.

46. Heikal, 169.

47. Lt Gen Saad el-Shazly, *The Crossing of the Suez* (San Francisco: American Mideast Research, 1980), 18.

48. Ibid., 25.

49. Ibid., 82.

50. Amos, 85.

51. Palit, 123.

52. "Arab Air Power, Part One," *Air International* 12 (June 1977): 294.

53. Amos, 93; Palit, 25.

54. Amos, 147, 156, 175; Nadav Safran, "Trial by Ordeal: The Yom Kippur War, October 1973," *International Security* 2, no. 2 (Fall 1977): 135-36.

55. Heikal, 265.

56. Ibid., 263.

57. Edgar O'Ballance, *No Victor, No Vanquished: The Yom Kippur War* (San Rafael, Calif.: Presidio Press, 1978), 34.

58. Glassman, 70.

59. Amos, 156; O'Ballance, *No Victor, No Vanquished*, 282.

60. Palit, 153.

61. Ibid., 154.

62. O'Ballance, *No Victor, No Vanquished*, 69.

63. Avraham (Bren) Adan, *On the Banks of the Suez* (San Rafael, Calif.: Presidio Press, 1980), 81.

64. O'Ballance, *No Victor, No Vanquished*, 86.

65. Ibid., 128

66. Safran, 52.

67. Adan, 384.

68. Palit, 87; O'Ballance, *No Victor, No Vanquished*, 134.

69. Shazly, 241.

70. Brig S. A. el-Edroos, *The Hashemite Arab Army, 1908-1979: An Appreciation and Analysis of Military Operations* (Amman, Jordan: The Publishing Committee and Fakenham, Norfolk, United Kingdom: Fakenham Press. Ltd., 1980), 534-36.

71. Palit, 156-57.

72. Martin van Crevald, "Military Lessons of the Yom Kippur War: Historical Perspectives" in Georgetown University Center for Strategic and International Studies, *The Washington Papers*, vol. 3, no. 24 (Beverly Hills: Sage Publications, 1975): 52.

73. Amos, op. cit., 212.

# CHAPTER 2

# Backgrounds of the IQAF and IIAF

## The Iraqi Air Force

The history of the Iraqi armed forces closely parallels the history of the modern Iraqi state since the armed forces have been a decisive force in the making and breaking of governments of that state. The area of Iraq (or Mesopotamia, the area of the Tigris and Euphrates Rivers) has been described through Arab history as difficult to govern.[1] It has always been a mosaic of antagonistic ethnic, religious, linguistic, and ideological groups. Prior to World War I, it had for centuries been ruled by the Ottoman Empire as the buffer between the Ottomans and the Persian Empire. The present-day state was a gerrymandered creation constructed for European imperial interests in the aftermath of World War I. Britain acquired it as a mandate chiefly to protect Imperial lines of communication to India.[2]

Although Iraqis had served in the Ottoman armies, the first Iraqi army was created in 1921. The Iraqi Air Force (IQAF) is the oldest Arab air force. It was established in 1931 as the Iraqi army's air arm and was equipped with five light aircraft to increase army effectiveness against dissident tribesmen.[3] This legacy of support for the army and concentration on internal security still continues. Until 1955, the IQAF was virtually an appendage of the RAF; its development was guided by the RAF and its aircraft were British.[4] With Iraq's entry into the Baghdad Pact in that year, British control lessened and then ceased after the 1958 revolution which ousted the monarchy which Britain had created in 1920 to rule with Iraq. Nonetheless, RAF aircraft remained based at Habbaniyah until 1959.[5]

In conjunction with the anti-imperialist aspect of the July 1958 revolution and in imitation of Nasser's example in Egypt, Iraq turned to the Soviet Union for military supplies. The first Soviet aircraft (MiG-17s and Il-28s) arrived 27 November 1958.[6] Though Soviet aid has continued to the present time, Soviet influence has waxed and waned as successive Baghdad governments have perceived a confluence or divergence of Soviet and Iraqi interests. Iraq moved closer to the Soviet Union after 1967 when it seemed to be the only way to counter Israeli strength and closer also in other periods such as when Iraqi forces engaged in open warfare with Kurdish immigrants and when a confident Iran pressured Baghdad over border issues—both circumstances which ceased in 1975.[7] The period from 1972 to 1975 marked the only extended period of broad and substantive cooperation between Baghdad and Moscow.

The periods of lesser cooperation often reflected Baghdad's displeasure with Soviet support for Iraqi communists.[8]

Iraq's ties with the West have remained fairly constant despite periodic anti-Western outbursts. Following the Baath* coup in February 1963, Iraq turned to Britain for Hawker Hunters and continued to deal with London through 1966, acquiring additional Hunters and Jet Provosts for use against Kurdish insurgents.[9] The militant anticommunism of this first Baath regime—it was ousted in November 1963—led Baghdad to pull Iraqi cadets out of Soviet training schools and to send them to Britain.[10] Baghdad, under the second Baath regime in 1968, also turned to France, seeking to acquire Mirages which had proved so successful in the Six-Day War. Although unsuccessful at that time, Iraq persevered and gained a French connection in 1977 with the purchase of 60 Mirage F-1s, the first of which arrived in Iraq in early 1981.[11]

Distrusting Soviet attempts to spread communist ideology among IQAF trainees, Baghdad also turned to India for training assistance. Iraqi pilots had received some training in India before the 1958 revolution. During the late 1960s and early 1970s, the Indian Air Force took over the training previously managed by the Soviets. Indian Air Force personnel were reputedly seconded to the IQAF to provide both flying and technical training. Despite the fluctuating nature of external ties, the IQAF remained very influenced by the RAF in its structure and traditions.[12]

## Wartime Combat Experience

IQAF combat experience has been limited when compared to the Egyptian and Syrian Air Forces. Iraq has always been a peripheral actor in the Arab-Israeli conflict, usually engaging the Israelis in a haphazard and uncoordinated fashion only after hostilities have begun. Iraqi air activity in 1948 was very limited and in 1956 was restricted to deployment of a few units to Jordan as a show of support. Iraq's 1967 experience included one abortive IQAF bomber raid on Israel (only one Tu-16 out of four made it to the target area where it hit the wrong target, caused little damage, and was shot down on egress) and one Israeli retaliatory raid on H-3 airfield in far western Iraq which destroyed 24 IQAF fighters. Israeli reports, however, credited the Iraqis with being the most aggressive of Arab pilots and said they had downed several Israelis in air-to-air combat.[13] The Iraqi army suffered, like other Arab armies in the Six-Day War, from Israeli air attack. An Iraqi column moving into Jordan was pounded for a day by Israeli aircraft, causing numerous casualties. The badly shattered unit never went into action.[14]

IQAF units operated on both the Suez and Golan fronts in the 1973 war and again Iraqi pilots received good marks for their performance. An Iraqi Hunter squadron

---

* Iraq's current (Fall 1982) government is controlled by the *Hizb al-Ba'ath al-Arabi al-Ishtiraki*, or the Arab Socialist Renaissance Party. It is referred to as the Baath Party in shortened form.

operating out of Egypt was used in the ground support role where, despite its reported good shooting (they apparently did a lot of strafing) and high morale, the entire squadron was eventually lost to Israeli air action.[15] Egyptian Chief of Staff Shazly, in his book, paid the Hunter pilots high praise.

> I pay particular tribute to the Iraqi Hunter pilots for the daring and skill of their anti-tank strikes in the Sinai. They swiftly gained such a reputation that our field commanders, calling for close air support, would frequently ask for the Iraqi squadron.[16]

The fact could not have been lost on the Iraqis, however, that pressing the attack in an arena where the enemy enjoyed air superiority is eventually a losing proposition.

Two Iraqi squadrons—joined later by an additional two squadrons—engaged in operations on the Syrian front where Iraq and Syria had an incredible lack of unity of effort and coordination. Like their army units on the Golan front, IQAF units were thrown into the fight as soon as they arrived. Some aircraft were lost to Syrian air defenses as some identification, friend or foe (IFF) systems (supposedly Su-7 systems, but more likely Hunters) reportedly were not integrated into the Syrian system.[17] While they had a poor concept of operations and next to no coordination with their allies, the Iraqis showed again that they would fight. But their valor was essentially wasted because of their organizational inadequacies.

## Political Influences

The impact of Iraqi domestic politics on the IQAF cannot be overstated. In October 1932, Iraq was the first Arab state to gain independence and was thereafter admitted to the League of Nations. In October 1936, Iraq had its first military coup, and the IQAF was an integral part of it. The leaders of this coup took power but were assassinated by other military men within a year. On six occasions between 1936 and 1941, military officer groups were decisive factors in deposing or appointing prime ministers either through the threat of or the actual use of force.[18] Through 1968, Iraq had seen a dozen military coups including the most important one, the 1958 revolution that turned the Iraqi government from a pro-Western monarchy into a radical, Pan-Arabist regime.[19]

Involvement in domestic politics has hurt Iraqi military professionalism. Majid Khadduri, a prominent Middle Eastern scholar, put it well when he noted that when the military becomes interested in politics, "actions as a soldier will always be subservient to politics."[20] Early in its existence, the Iraqi military realized it could be the ultimate power broker in the state and consequently political intrigue became more important to the officer corps than military professionalism. The Iraqi army's abject failure in fighting against British troops in 1941 was a result of five years of political

21

maneuvering in which the army had gone from an instrument of power for the state to an instrument for power within the state.[21]

This heavy involvement with politics has also been disastrous for continuity within the Iraqi military. Of all Iraqi political leaders since 1958, 28 percent have come from the military academy.[22] Yet each coup since 1958 has resulted in purges of those military men thought closely associated with the losing side in the coup. After Gen Abdul Karim Qassem's 1958 coup, every general was purged.[23] From 1958 to February 1963 when Qassem himself was overthrown and killed, he executed, imprisoned, or removed 2,000 of 8,000 total officers. By 1967, Iraqi armed forces' morale had not yet recovered from these purges.[24] Although the present government has held on since 1968, purges have continued—for instance 300 officers were purged after a 1970 coup attempt.[25] The air force has played a major part in these upheavals. The first Baathist coup in February 1963 was led by a group of air force officers based at Habbaniyah. Air force aircraft bombed the Defense Ministry building in Baghdad until General Qassem surrendered.[26] The Baathists were then ousted within the year. In 1965, the air force failed in a second coup attempt.[27] Each time, more "disloyal" officers were weeded out. A military coup attempt backed by the Iraqi Communist Party in 1978 led to another extensive purge of the high command, and the IQAF was put under close Baath Party control.[28]

The current Baathist regime seems to have learned the lesson of too much military involvement. The Baath leadership is dominated by its civilian wing that has put the Baathist stamp on the military, especially the air force. Much of the top Baath leadership comes from the town of Tikrit, and many of the 1963 coup plotters were Tikriti military men.[29] Since 1933, the IQAF has had its own college as a source of officers. In 1971, the college was moved from Rashid (a Baghdad suburb) to Tikrit,[30] an obvious effort to get air force cadets away from the political setting of the capital and into the home of Baath leadership where a watchful eye could be kept on them. The Baath has not neglected follow-on professional military education. The course at the National Defense College was developed, according to its dean,

> for the purpose of training and preparing the vanguard leaders and the elements who will be candidates for positions of leadership in the [Baath] Party, in the army, and in the sensitive state offices, with the most advanced and modern knowledge and studies on the revolutionary [read Baath] view of the concept of the job of national defense.[31]

Loyalty to the Baath regime, not necessarily professional ability, is the prerequisite for advancement in the IQAF and military.

## Organization and Mission

The key fact about the IQAF and its role in Iraqi military thought is that it has been and is subservient to the army. Initially, it was set up as the army air arm to increase the army's ability to maintain internal security and today remains subordinate to the army with the Air Force commander reporting to the army chief of staff. A 1968 area handbook noted that "part of the army [author's emphasis] [the IQAF] is charged with providing air support for ground forces and assisting in air defense."[32] Nothing has changed. While the IQAF may not be effective at supporting the army and may not be called on very often in this role, its subservient position is a reflection of Iraqi opinion that the army is the decisive military arm.

As the war with Iran opened, this was the IQAF's order of battle. In the air defense role, the IQAF operated the radar and aircraft portions of the system while the army operated the SAMs (unlike in Egypt where the ground-based Air Defense Command is a separate service). Ten thousand of the 38,000 IQAF personnel were dedicated to the air defense mission.[33] Each interceptor squadron was deployed at a separate base for defense of a specific target. Their five interceptor squadrons had limited all-weather capability and were all equipped with MiG-21s. In the ground support role, the IQAF provided aircraft for close air support and strike roles and, to a limited extent, for air superiority over the immediate battlefield.[34] In 1980, the IQAF had 12 ground attack squadrons—4 equipped with MiG-23Bs, 3 with Su-7Bs, 4 with Su-20s, and 1 with Hawker Hunters. Additionally, the IQAF had two bomber squadrons equipped with Tu-22s and Il-28s respectively—though the latter were probably inoperable—and two transport squadrons whose primary aircraft were Il-76s and An-12s. The 11 helicopter squadrons included attack helicopters like Soviet Mi-8s and Mi-24s as well as western European-designed and -built Alouettes, Pumas, Gazelles, and Super Frelons.[35]

Thus, the IQAF's mission was essentially supportive and defensive. Against Israel, the IQAF was prepared to support frontline Arab states. Against Iran, the IQAF remained fairly defensive, recognizing that its aircraft with their shorter ranges and smaller payloads were at a disadvantage when compared to Iran's F-4 and F-5 fleet which were also augmented by an aerial refueling capability.

## The Iranian Air Force

The Islamic Iranian Air Force of 1980 did not have the long historical tradition of the IQAF. In a real sense, it was mostly a product of former President Richard M. Nixon's 1972 decision to allow the shah to buy whatever he wanted from US defense contractors.[36] Before that time, the IIAF had been a relatively small affair with its most sophisticated aircraft being 129 F-5A/B fighters provided in the late 1960s and early 1970s, largely under the grant Military Assistance Program (MAP).[37] Although the IIAF had always been associated solely with American aircraft and American assistance, from 1972 forward, increasing US aircraft sales and US Air Force assistance helped the IIAF grow into almost a mirror image of the United States Air Force.

The American aid and assistance tie reflected a historical pattern for the Iranian military. Iran has a very old national and military tradition; but by the start of the nineteenth century, Iranian leaders could see that Russian pressure from the north and British pressure from the south were threatening to overwhelm Iran's independence. One way to resist these pressures was to seek out the assistance of a third party who would help Iran modernize its armed forces. The first foreign advisers arrived in Iran in 1809. By 1845, Iran was sending a few military men to Europe for study. Throughout the rest of the nineteenth century, Iran sought military advisory assistance from Italy, France, Austria-Hungary, and Russia. The first modernized formation that took root in the Iranian military was the Russian-advised Persian Cossack Brigade. Formed in 1879, it had by 1896 become an imperial guard for the shahs of the Qajar dynasty.[38] In February 1921, Reza Khan, head of the Cossack Brigade, overthrew the government in a coup d'état. In 1925, he deposed the Qajars and became the first of the two Pahlavi shahs.[39] The close tie between the military and the Pahlavi shah was born.

Reza Khan's son, Mohammed Reza, became the shah during World War II when the allies forced his pro-German father to abdicate. The new shah began immediately after the war to try to build up the Iranian armed forces, a quite illogical step since the Soviet Union occupied the northern part of Iran and there was a genuine threat of a total Soviet takeover. The Iran-US military tie began at that time.[40] A US military advisory mission to the Iranian gendarmerie had been established in 1942. The following year, one was established with the Iranian army as well. In 1947, the United States began to extend credit to the then nearly destitute Iran so that it could buy US war surplus equipment. This evolved through the 1950s into a mutual defense assistance program through which the United States provided grant military aid to the Iranian armed forces. During the period of grant aid, the shah generally tried to gain more military aid than the United States thought necessary or prudent.[41] It was obvious that the shah thought Iran needed more equipment. In his 1961 autobiography *Mission for My Country*, he pointed out Iran's vital position as a bulwark against Soviet expansion. He also mentioned Iraq's large military and noted: "Our armed forces—and especially our air force—are weak and suffer from lack of the most modern equipment." He noted the IIAF, at that time, was "a small air force designed mainly for providing support for our ground forces in limited actions."[42]

As Iran's increasing oil revenues gave the shah the ability to buy the arms he wanted, the picture changed. After Britain withdrew from the Gulf in 1971, the Nixon Doctrine envisioned Iran and Saudi Arabia—the "twin pillars"—filling the power vacuum in the area. To allow Iran to play that role, the shah was encouraged to build up his armed forces through purchases of American equipment. The shah took up the offer with a vengeance. His style was to buy early, many, and the best. He bought early and bought the best in an attempt to improve Iran's fledgling defense industry by buying access to technology when Iran had great leverage. He bought many as a hedge against resupply problems if a war resulted in rapid attrition rates. And he bought strictly US combat aircraft in an attempt to gain implicit US support for Iran's security, the third party support that had been the foundation of Iranian foreign policy for the last century and a half.

Although the shah tried from 1973 on to proceed with vast expansion and modernization programs for all the services, the IIAF was the most favored service. It received the largest share of defense modernization expenditures and had less trouble than the other services in finding and retaining qualified personnel. From 1970 to 1977, the IIAF increased in numbers of personnel from 17,000 to 100,000 and in numbers of combat aircraft from 175 to 341. But such growth was not without problems. Sophisticated aircraft came into the inventory faster than air and ground crews could be trained. So much equipment was bought so fast that the American side of the exchange could not adequately account for all the transactions. Most of the critics of the US-Iranian arms relationship seemed to focus on the size of the shah's purchasing in relation to Iran's threat. They felt he could never have enough to hold off the Soviets, but he was buying far more than he needed to defend Iran from any regional enemies.[43] The shah, however, recognized that Iran needed a strong air force to serve as a deterrent to Iraqi ambitions. To protect Iran from air attacks on valuable targets, the shah bought aircraft and air defense equipment to both protect Iran and to give it at least a comparable capability to retaliate. The IIAF was the deterrent.[44] By 1978, however, Iran had an "awesome potential in terms of airpower."[45] In addition to the quantities of aircraft bought, the quality of the systems meant the IIAF was overwhelmingly the most powerful regional air force. Although the IIAF had no real combat experience, US Air Force training—both in the United States and inside Iran—was probably realistic enough to make up for some of the combat experience shortcomings. The IQAF did not have much to show for all its experience in combat, while the IIAF was receiving the benefit of US Air Force experiences against Soviet systems. The shah had hoped the IIAF would have been among the finest in the world by 1982.[46]

But the IIAF, under the shah, was not a pure, independent military organization. Various students of Iranian politics noted that the shah's concern with the security of his crown led him to exercise "leadership by distrust."[47] The IIAF was one of the various groupings inside Iranian politics that the shah manipulated; everything centered on him and he balanced one group off against the other. There was, for example, no joint service planning.[48] The shah, as supreme commander of Iran's military forces, exercised direct operational control over the services. The IIAF commander, like the other service chiefs, reported directly to the shah; the minister of war and the supreme commander's staff were not in the chain of command. Loyalty to the shah was the primary basis for advancement and several cross-checking security organizations constantly gauged the loyalty of all key military figures. The shah reportedly studied the record of every man recommended for promotion above the rank of major.[49] In this environment of suspicion and distrust, individual initiative suffered and tight centralized control was the norm.[50]

Much of this was nonapplicable by the fall of 1980, however. The senior command echelon of the IIAF had been decapitated in 1979 and early 1980 by arrests, imprisonments, executions, purges, and forced exiles. A failed coup that originated on Shahrokhi Air Base in Hamadan in June 1980 brought about another sweeping purge. Many IIAF personnel were shot or jailed for suspected or real complicity in the coup attempt, and the purge of personnel whose ultimate loyalty was suspect continued at a faster pace. Iraq's attack forced the abol Hasan Bani-Sadr government to free some pilots from prison so that they could fly missions in defense of their country (and their jailers as well).[51]

While the turbulence continued in the command and personnel structure through the summer of 1980, the IIAF aircraft force structure remained potent at the time of the Iraqi attack. The IIAF had 77 F-14As for the air defense role, though their ability to use the Phoenix missile was questionable. The backbone of the force was its 166 F-4Ds and Es. All the F-4Es had leading edge slats for increased maneuverability, some were capable of firing the Maverick air-to-ground missile, and others had an electro-optical target identification system. The 166 F-5Es and Fs were quite capable ground attack fighters and effective good weather interceptors. Additionally, the IIAF had KC-707 tankers for aerial refueling, Boeing 747s and 707s for strategic airlift, and C-130s for tactical airlift.[52] Despite the political turmoil, the IIAF in late 1980 was still a force not to be trifled with.

## NOTES

1. Majid Khadduri, *Arab Contemporaries: The Role of Personalities in Politics* (Baltimore: Johns Hopkins University Press, 1973), 31.

2. R. D. McLaurin, Mohammed Mughisuddin, and Abraham R. Wagner, *Foreign Policy Making in the Middle East: Domestic Influences on Policy in Egypt, Iraq, Israel, and Syria* (New York: Praeger, 1977), 108; Mark Heller, "Politics and the Military in Iraq and Jordan, 1920-1958: The British Influence," *Armed Forces and Society* 4 (November 1977): 77.

3. "Arab Air Power, Part Two," *Air International* 13 (July 1977): 7; Harvey H. Smith et al., *Area Handbook for Iraq* (Washington, D.C.: Government Printing Office, 1969), 340–41.

4. "Arab Air Power, Part Two," 8.

5. SIPRI, 556.

6. Ibid.

7. Francis Fukuyama, *The Soviet Union and Iraq Since 1968*, Rand Note N-1524-AF prepared for the US Air Force, (Santa Monica, Calif.: Rand, July 1980), 30, 38.

8. Ibid., v-vi.

9. "Arab Air Power, Part Two," 7; SIPRI, 220.

10. SIPRI, 557.

11. Ibid., 256; Frank J. Prime, "France Confirms Report It Has Handed Over 4 Mirage Jets to Iraqis," *NYT*, 2 February 1981, A6.

12. "Arab Air Power, Part Two," 7; Richard F. Nyrop, ed., *Iraq: A Country Study* (Washington, D.C.: American University, 1979), 244.

13. Geisenheyner, 47-48; O'Ballance, *Third Arab-Israeli War*, 83.

14. Edgar O'Ballance, *The Kurdish Revolt: 1961–1970* (Hamden, Conn.: Archon Books, 1973), 143.

15. Palit, 155–56; "The Iraqi Baath Party II," *Le Matin An-Nahar Arab Report* 5 (11 November 1974).

16. Shazly, 278.

17. Ibid.; Palit, 109; "Arab Air Power, Part Two," 7.

18. Eliezar Be'eri, *Army Officers in Arab Politics and Society* (New York: Frederick A. Praeger, Inc., 1970), 15–16, 35.

19. Majid Khadduri, *Political Trends in the Arab World: The Role of Ideas and Ideals in Politics* (Baltimore: Johns Hopkins University Press, 1970), 134.

20. Ibid., 141.

21. Be'eri, 39.

22. Phebe A. Marr, "The Political Elite in Iraq," *Political Elites in the Middle East*, ed. George Lenczowski (Washington, D.C.: American Enterprise Institute, 1975), 116.

23. Heller, 84.

24. O'Ballance, *Third Arab-Israeli War*, 179.

25. Fukuyama, 31.

26. O'Ballance, *The Kurdish Revolt*, 96–97.

27. Ibid., 130.

28. Anthony H. Cordesman, "Lessons of the Iran-Iraq War: The First Round," *Armed Forces Journal International* 119 (April 1982): 42.

29. John F. Devlin, *The Ba'th Party: A History from Its Origins to 1966* (Stanford, Calif.: Hoover Institution Press, 1976), 233.

30. Nyrop, 243.

31. Ibid., 244.

32. Smith, 342.

33. *The Military Balance 1980–1981* (London: The International Institute for Strategic Studies, 1980), 43 (hereafter referred to as *IISS 80–81*).

34. "Arab Air Power, Part Two," 8–9.

35. *IISS 80-81*, 42.

36. Yonah Alexander and Allan Nanes, eds., *The United States and Iran: A Documentary History.* (Frederick, Md.: University Publications of America, 1980), 405–6.

37. Senate, Committee on Foreign Relations, Subcommittee on Foreign Assistance, *US Military Sales to Iran*, 94th Cong., 2d sess., Staff Report, July 1976, 30.

38. J. C. Hurewitz, *Middle East Politics: The Military Dimension* (New York: Praeger, 1969), 40–41.

39. Nikki R. Keddie, *Iran: Religion, Politics and Society* (Totowa, N.J.: Frank Cass & Co., Ltd., 1980), 213.

40. House, Committee on International Relations, *United States Arms Sales to the Persian Gulf*, 94th Cong., 1st sess., January 1976, Study Mission Report Pursuant to H. Res. 315, January 1976, 115–64.

41. Barry Rubin, *Paved with Good Intentions: The American Experience and Iran* (New York: Oxford University Press, 1980), 38.

42. Mohammad Reza Shah Pahlavi, *Mission for my Country* (New York: McGraw–Hill Book Co., 1961), 309–16.

43. Extensive discussion of this period can be found in Theodore Moran, "Iranian Defense Expenditures and the Social Crisis," *International Security* 3, no. 3 (Winter 1978–1979): 178–92; Stephanie Neuman, "Security, Military Expenditures and Socioeconomic Development: Reflections on Iran," *Orbis* 22, no. 3

(Fall 1978): 569–94; Shahram Chubin. "Iran's Security in the 1980s." *International Security* 2 (Winter 1978): 51–80; and Senate. *US Military Sales to Iran*. 30.

44. Robert J. Pranger and Dale R. Tahtinen. "American Policy Options in Iran and the Persian Gulf." *AEI Foreign Policy and Defense Review* 1. no. 2 (1979): 13–14.

45. Steven L. Canby and Edward N. Luttwak. *The Control of Arms Transfers and Perceived Security Needs* (Report prepared by C&L Assoc.. Potomac. Md.. for US Arms Control and Disarmament Agency). 14 April 1980. 143.

46. Mohammad Reza Shah Pahlavi. *Answer to History* (New York: Stern and Day. 1980). 142.

47. Khosrow Fatemi. "Leadership by Distrust: The Shah's *Modus Operandi.*" *Middle East Journal* 36. no. 1 (Winter 1982): 48.

48. Rubin. *Paved with Good Intentions*. 169.

49. William H. Forbis. *Fall of the Peacock Throne: The Story of Iran* (New York: Harper and Row. Publishers. Inc.. 1980). 281.

50. See also James A. Bill. "Iran and the Crisis of '78." *Foreign Affairs* 52. no. 2 (Winter 1978–1979): 323–42; Bill. *The Politics of Iran: Groups. Classes. and Modernization* (Columbus. Ohio: Charles E. Merrill Publishing Co.. 1972); House. Committee on International Relations. *United States Arms Policies in the Persian Gulf and Red Sea Areas: Past. Present. and Future*. 95th Cong.. 1st sess.. December 1977. Staff Survey Mission Report Pursuant to H. Res. 313. 123–24.

51. "War Developments." *Aviation Week and Space Technology* 113 (hereafter referred to as AWST) (20 October 1980): 31.

52. House. *United States Arms Sales to the Persian Gulf*. 28–31; *IISS 80-81*. 42.

# CHAPTER 3

# Reasons for the War

"Initially we were happy to see the fall of the Shah."[1] So said a Baath Party official in a 1981 interview. Indeed they were. The shah had taken upon himself the role of policeman of the Gulf; and with purchases of huge quantities of American weapons, he had the military force to back up his stance. The Imperial armed forces had flexed their muscle in April 1969 when the shah decided to alter the status quo on the Shatt-al-Arab, the river that forms the lower border between Iran and Iraq. Imperial Iranian Navy gunboats and IIAF fighters escorted Iranian shipping up the Shatt-al-Arab to back up the shah's unilateral abrogation of a 1937 treaty that had given sovereignty of the river to Iraq.[2] Iraq felt it could not, at that time, take on the shah; and six years later, the Baathist government was forced to publicly concede that Iraq was not the sole owner of the Shatt-al-Arab. The 1975 Algiers Accords gave both countries equal ownership of the river.[3] While photographs of the signing show smiles all around, there was considerable doubt that Iraqi strongman Saddam Husayn's joy over the treaty was genuine. The collapse of the Pahlavi dynasty must have felt like sweet revenge to Husayn and the Baath leadership.

Iraq and Iran experienced a cooperative *modus vivendi* from 1975 to 1979, and Baghdad had every reason to expect it would continue as the revolutionary Iranian regime sorted out its internal problems. Events during the summer of 1979 ended this period of reconciliation. Iraq, concerned that Iranian Kurdish insurrection against the Tehran regime might spill over the border and spark renewed Iraqi Kurdish problems, carried out some intimidation-style military operations along the border in Kurdistan, including some IQAF bombing of villages just inside Iran. Iran's response was not only condemnation of the raids but also to accuse Baghdad of oppressing its Shia* Muslim citizens.[4]

Iraq's Baathist leaders must have known problems with Iran were inevitable. They knew that they already had three strikes against them with Khomeini, and as a favor to the shah, in 1978 they kicked him out of Iraq where he had lived as an exile for 14 years. Second, the Shias in Iraq were definite second-class citizens. And third, Baath Party ideology was determinedly secular, relegating Islam to the status of a private choice of conscience; a historical and cultural influence rather than a total, all-encompassing way of life as Khomeini saw it.[5] In stark contrast to Khomeini's

---

* Without getting into theological differences, it is most important to recognize that Shia Islam is the official state religion of Iran. Two of the most important Shia religious sites, however, are inside Iraq. About 55 percent of Iraqi citizens are Shia Muslims, but the Iraqi government historically has been dominated by Sunni Muslims.

vision of the perfect society, Iraq's public society in 1979 and 1980 was marked by a bare deference to religion, a public role for emancipated women and a decided preference for modernism over Islam.[6]

The invective between Tehran and Baghdad became serious in the early summer of 1979. Unable to compete with Iran's championing of the Islamic cause, Iraq took up the banner of Arabism. In June, Baath Party newspapers revived the Arab grievance against the shah's taking of three Arab islands near the Strait of Hormuz—the Greater and Lesser Tunbs and Abu Musa. The Iraqis also began to warn Iran about acting like the shah who, in the past, had threatened the Arabs.[7] Surreptitiously, Iraq began to give aid and encouragement to autonomy-seeking Iranian Arabs residing in the Iranian oil province of Khuzistan. Shortly thereafter, a wave of sabotage incidents occurred.[8]

In October, the mutual antipathy increased when Iraq, which had already reopened the Abu Musa-Tunbs wound, resurfaced an even more serious one—the Shatt-al-Arab issue. In the same statement, Iraq also voiced support for autonomy-seeking Iranian minorities, a direct threat to the integrity of any Iranian state—Islamic Republic or otherwise.[9] Iranian invective concentrated on religion, with Iranian clergymen openly inciting Iraqi Shiites to overthrow their Baathist (and Sunni) rulers.

On 1 April 1980, a would-be assassin threw a grenade at Iraq's Deputy Premier Tariq Aziz in Baghdad. Iraq claimed the assailant, who was killed, was an Iranian and accused Tehran of sponsoring terrorist groups inside Iraq. Baghdad took the incident as an opportunity to clean up a few of its own problems and to inflict a few more on Tehran by forcing thousands of persons of Iranian origin out of Iraq and across the Iranian border.[10] (The expulsions were a ritualistic way for Baghdad to show displeasure with Tehran. Between one-half and 1 million Iranian Shias have lived in Iraq for generations. Calling their action the deportation of illegal aliens, Iraqi authorities had expelled 20,000 in 1969 in reaction to the shah's aforementioned abrogation of the 1937 Shatt-al-Arab treaty and had deported 60,000 more in 1971 after the shah had seized Abu Musa and the Tunbs.)[11] By this time, the leaders of both countries were calling for the other's overthrow. Khomeini predicted the Baath regime would be "thrown into the dustbin of history." Husayn said Khomeini was "another shah" disguised in a turban and that Iran was governed by a bunch of dictators who should be replaced.[12]

In late August and early September, border clashes—which had been intermittent for some time—began to intensify. *Keyhan,* a Tehran newspaper, warned on 25 August that Iraqi aircraft were preparing to attack western Iranian provinces.[13] On 6 September, *Keyhan* reported 48 hours of fierce fighting along the central border region.[14] Fighting seemed to be going on in an area from Qasr-e Shirin south to Mehran, a strip that had been in contention for years. Both Baghdad and Tehran began to broadcast exaggerated claims of success. Iraq claimed to have "liberated" first 76, then 210, square kilometers of disputed territory.[15] Almost daily, Tehran radio began to report heavy fighting, often including the use of helicopters on both sides. IIAF fighters were reported engaging both in ground support roles and in air-to-air engagements.

On 17 September, Iraq declared the Algiers Accord on borders null and void and moved to assert its control over the Shatt as well as the disputed central border areas.[16] (Reflecting the indiscipline in the Tehran government at that time, Iranian Armed Forces Chief of Staff General Fallahi agreed with Baghdad when he said, "We do not recognize the 1975 Algiers agreement concluded by Iraq and Iran concerning the land borders.")[17] On 20 September, Iran recalled to service a number of former military personnel.[18] About the same time, Arab diplomats were saying that Iraq, having gained its border objectives, was now preparing for Iranian counterattacks.[19] Continuation of the increasingly nasty and expensive border clashes appeared likely. On the 22d, however, Iranian President Bani-Sadr said over Tehran radio that "Saddam Husayn today tried to imitate [sic] Moshe Dayan to attack our airports."[20]

## The Reasons

What had impelled Iraq to take this action? Why did it launch a war on Iran, a country with three times Iraq's population and almost four times its size? That Baghdad was provoked is beyond doubt, but what reasoning lay behind what now, two years later, looks like a tragically flawed decision?

Early in the conflict, a Pakistani observer gave us an apt insight when he said that the war had gotten the better of sound reason and professional judgment and had become a vendetta; that it had become less a war than a mass suicide with no hope of salvage.[21]

It is doubtful that we shall ever know Baghdad's exact calculation or precise goals for launching its assault on Iran. The leadership in Baghdad may well have had only a hazy idea of its original goals; but as problem has succeeded problem, regime survival has become the top priority. It appears, however, that there were three general attitudes that motivated Baghdad to use the military option. First, Iraq saw itself as the emergent power in the Persian Gulf area. Second, the Iraqi leadership was nurturing some past grievances against Tehran and could see the opportunity to avenge them. And third, the Islamic regime of Ayatollah Khomeini was presenting a definite ideological challenge to the rulers in Baghdad. Self-preservation, above all, is vital to any group of leaders.

For years, Iraq had a reputation as the odd-man out, the archradical, the rejectionist, the fomenter of revolution; but by 1980, it acquired a new-found respectability. Its economy was thriving. The nationalization of the Iraqi oil industry in 1972 had given the government direct control over that vital source of income, one that became increasingly valuable as the Organization of Petroleum Exporting Countries (OPEC) enforced its price structure during the 1970s. The amount of money devoted to public expenditures increased as the Baath government sought to modernize, but not at the frenetic pace of the shah's Iran. The amount of money in Iraqi private hands had increased, but strict government control had kept inflation in check. Iraq's economic outlook was promising.[22]

The leadership in Baghdad felt fairly secure. After experiencing one major revolution, three successful coups, a civil war, and a number of aborted coups in the decade after 1958, Iraq had since 1968 been under the control of the Baath Party. Saddam Husayn had been the offstage power controlling the government since 1968, and in 1979 ascended to formal power when he became president after the retirement of former President Ahmed Hassan al-Bakr. Immediately after he became president, Husayn's security apparatus detected and crushed an attempted coup against him. After personally overseeing the execution of 21 of the top governmental leadership and cowing other potential rivals, Husayn felt secure. So secure, in fact, that he allowed Iraq to hold elections for a rubber-stamp assembly. This was patently designed to burnish the image of Baath control. He also made an attempt to develop a personality cult making publicized tours all through the country and appearing often on television and at parties all over the country.[23] Meanwhile, Baghdad had kept its chronic Kurdish problems under control through a combination of moves including force, relocation, and economic incentives. In short, there existed in Baghdad in the summer of 1980 a confident Baath leadership, fairly certain it would not fall to a coup.

With a prosperous economy and a fairly secure power base as a backdrop, Iraq had begun by 1978 to move out of its isolation in the Arab world. Arab disenchantment with the Camp David Treaty opened the door for Iraq to try for a leadership role in the Arab world—as part of the millenia-old rivalry between the Nile River Valley and Mesopotamia. To help achieve this goal, the radical revolutionary Baathists suddenly adopted a moderate, live-and-let-live public face. The Baghdad Summit meeting, held in November 1978 to determine an Arab strategy to cope with Egypt's move toward peace, illuminated the willingness of conservative and moderate Arab states to accept Baathist Iraq into their fold. Baghdad dropped its wild-man attitudes and became the champion of the status quo. Iraq and Saddam Husayn's growing regional and international stature culminated when Baghdad was chosen as the site of the 1982 Non-Aligned Conference with Husayn becoming president-elect of the Non-Aligned Movement. This was quite an accomplishment for a man who in 1959 was an unsuccessful political assassin, digging a bullet out of his leg as he fled in a getaway car.

The year 1979 also marked the exit of Iraq's chief rival for Gulf supremacy—the Pahlavi dynasty in Iran. The shah's demise left a leadership vacuum in the Gulf. Irritated as they were by the shah's pretensions, the Arabian Peninsula states had been able to live with him as he had generally been a force for royal stability. The erratic, follow-on government in Tehran guaranteed to be a destabilizing influence, much like Iraq had been in the past. With Iran stewing, Iraq had only to appear moderate to look attractive. Putting on its moderate face, Baghdad boldly offered to take up the mantle of Gulf leadership. By the summer of 1980, Baghdad felt secure as—in its eyes at least—the Gulf's leader and protector, ready to discipline any local state who threatened the prosperity and tranquility of the area.[24]

Both Saddam Husayn and his government in Baghdad had a score to settle with Tehran over border issues. Ever since the area of Iraq had been the uneasy border between the Ottoman and Persian Empires, the conflicting border claims have led to boundary disputes. What has not been in dispute, however, is that force has usually prevailed in these disagreements. No matter what the legalistic form border settlements took, the side which had the perceived preponderance of military strength usually got its way. By the fall of 1980, Iraq could feel the military power pendulum swinging its way. Iran's armed forces were mostly American equipped and trained; but with Iran holding American diplomats hostage, Washington was unlikely to do anything to help the Iranian military should it need it. Iran's military disintegration was widely advertised. The Indian journal *Strategic Analysis* in June 1980 reported Iranian military morale was extremely low—especially in the IIAF—manpower was being cut by over 50 percent, and billions of dollars' worth of equipment was useless due to parts shortages.[25] A Pakistani observer noted that anyone who got his information from the Western press would have concluded that Iraq had military superiority.[26] The Iraqis were probably also getting this information from "official" sources since they reportedly had informal contacts with European and US intelligence services.[27] Baghdad was also getting information from Iranian exile groups that doubtlessly were informing the Iraqis that their failed coup at Shahrokhi Air Base in June had caused another wave of executions and purges, further weakening the IIAF.[28] The exiles, too, were probably assuring Baghdad that the Iranian people were just waiting for outside assistance so they would rise up and overthrow the Islamic Republic. Mention of the Islamic Republic brings up the third, and probably most vital, reason—the ideological challenge of Khomeini to the Baathist regime.

Iraq is a notoriously difficult country to govern. While Iraqi society is rent with the normal cleavages extant in all Middle Eastern countries (urban-rural, modern-traditional, etc.), the most significant ones are along ethnic and religious lines. Twenty percent of Iraq's population consists of Sunni Muslim Kurd, a group not particularly fond of the central government. Fifty to 55 percent is Shia Muslim Arab, while 5 percent is non-Muslim or other non-Arab. The remaining 20 or so percent is Sunni Muslim Arab. This last group is the dominant force in Iraq; it runs the government and the economy. The largest element of the population, the Shia community, is more or less excluded from these two areas. Also, they are, in general, more traditional and are thus disposed to listen to Shia mullahs for guidance who, in turn, look to Iran for guidance.[29] In contrast, the secular Arabism of the Baath (which was originally formulated to attract both Christian and Muslim Arabs) is an attempt to unify Arabs along ideological lines rather than allowing them to be divided along religious ones. Thus, Iran's calls for Islamic revolution are a direct ideological challenge to secular Baath Arabism just as Radio Tehran's castigation of Saddam

33

Husayn is a direct personal threat to him. Tehran's calls for Islamic revolution were also a threat to any other Middle Eastern rulers not seen as representing Islamic law, whether by Iran or by their own people. As such, many of the rulers on the Gulf felt the Iranian challenge, and they were not averse to allowing Iraq to stifle that challenge. Thus, Baghdad could eliminate the threat to itself which, in turn, would help Iraq assume the mantle of Arab leadership. Conversely, of course, an inability to eliminate the Khomeini threat would put in doubt these leadership pretensions.[30]

Information at Baghdad's disposal made Iran seem ripe to fall. The hostage issue had isolated Iran from most of the world, and for once Iraq found itself more respectable in the world's eyes. Baghdad calculated that neither Washington nor Moscow, for different reasons, would mind Khomeini's demise and neither was likely to step in to save him. Undoubtedly, none of the Arab states Iraq wished to lead would mind the removal of the Khomeini threat. In the final analysis, Iraq had some grievances with Iran, but they did not necessarily mean war. But Iraq was in 1980 still in the process of stepping out of the shadows of political isolation. It was at the point where it could step up to Gulf, as well as Arab and Third World, leadership. Iraq, therefore, had to put down this ideological challenge and in September 1980 the odds looked good for Baghdad. The Iraqi military would undertake a nice little war that a weakened Iranian military could not effectively counter with the result that Khomeini's house of cards would collapse, and Saddam Husayn would be the savior of Arab royalists and republicans alike. Ignoring Iran's provocations, the ambitions of Iraq's leaders would remain stillborn.

# NOTES

1. Fred Halliday, "Interviews—Ba'th Command: 'Initially We Were Happy to See the Fall of the Shah'," *MERIP Reports* 97, June 1981, 19-21.

2. Robert D. Tomasek, "The Resolution of Major Controversies between Iran and Iraq," *World Affairs* 139, no. 3 (Winter 1976-1977): 206-14.

3. "Iran-Iraq: Treaty on International Borders and Good Neighborly Relations," *International Legal Materials* 14 (September 1975): 1133-38.

4. See the "Chronology" section of the *Middle East Journal*, vols. 32-34.

5. Kamel S. Abu Jabar, *The Arab Ba'th Socialist Party: History, Ideology, and Organization* (Syracuse, N.Y.: Syracuse University Press, 1966), vii, 129.

6. Wayne Morrison, "Iraq: Little Islam, Much Modernism," *Asiaweek* 6 (19 September 1980): 30.

7. R. S. Thapar, "Iran-Iraq Border Confrontation," *Strategic Analysis* 3, no. 5 (August 1979): 193.

8. For example, the *Middle East Journal* "Chronology" shows: 7 July 1979—explosion damages two pipelines to Abadan refinery; 30 September 1979—microwave station blown up in southwest Iran; 3 October 1979—bomb on a train near Khorramshahr; 6 October 1979—pipeline explosion near Ahwaz; 19 December 1979—pipeline explosion near Dezfūl.

9. R. S. Thapar, "Iran-Iraq Conflict," *Strategic Analysis* 4, no. 2 (May 1980): 66.

10. "Armies of Iran and Iraq Go on Alert as Baghdad Expels 7,000 Iranians," *Wall Street Journal* (hereafter referred to as *WSJ*), 8 April 1980, 3.

11. Tomasek, 211-12.

12. Thapar, "Iran-Iraq Conflict," 62-63.

13. "Daily Report, South Asia" (Washington, D.C.: Foreign Broadcast Information Service) (hereafter referred to as *FBIS-SAS - 80* ), vol. 8, 25 August 1980, Tehran newspaper *Keyhan* in Persian.

14. "Reports of 48 hours Fierce Fighting," *FBIS-SAS-80*, 6 September 1980, Tehran newspaper *Keyhan* in Persian.

15. "Iran-Iraq Clashes Intensity," *Middle East Economic Digest* 24, no. 37 (hereafter referred to as *MEED*) (12 September 1980): 13; "Algiers Agreement Declared Null," *MEED* 23, no. 38 (19 September 1980): 33.

16. "Iraq Ends 1975 Border Pact with Iran as Frontier Clashes Continue," *NYT*, 18 September 1980, A8.

17. "Algier's Agreement Declared Null," *MEED*, 19 September 1980, 33.

18. "Recall of Former Military Personnel," *FBIS-SAS-80*, Tehran radio broadcast in Persian dated 1634 GMT, 20 September 1980.

19. Werner Wiskari, "Iraq Said to Gain Its Border Aims in Iran Conflict," *NYT*, 20 September 1980, 1.

20. "Bani-Sadr Speech," *FBIS-SAS-80*, Tehran radio broadcast in Persian dated 1525 GMT, 22 September 1980.

21. Brig Abdul Rahman Siddiqi, "The Gulf War of Attrition," *Defence Journal* (Karachi, Pakistan) 6, no. 10 (1980): 1-10; Siddiqi, "The Gulf's Wanton War," *Defence Journal* (Karachi, Pakistan) 6, no. 11 (1980): 1-10.

22. Joe Stork, "Iraq and the War in the Gulf," *MERIP Reports* 97, June 1981, 3-18; Basil al-Bustany, "Iraq: Economic Developments," *AEI Foreign Policy and Defense Review* 2 (1980): 38-44.

23. Claudia Wright, "Iraq—New Power in the Middle East," *Foreign Affairs* 58 (Winter 1979-1980): 257-77; Wright, "The Strong Men of the Arab World," *Maclean's* 93 (30 June 1980): 26-27; Bill Paul, "Who is Real Hussein—the Genial Jekyll or Hideous Hyde?" *WSJ*, 13 June 1980, 1.

24. Bill Paul, "Iraq's Ambitions: Baghdad Seeks to Use Oil to Gain Influence, Shed Its Radical Image," *WSJ*, 4 June 1980, 1; Adeed I. Dawisha, "Iraq: The West's Opportunity," *Foreign Policy*, Winter 1980-1981, 143.

25. Sreedhar, "State of Iranian Armed Forces," *Strategic Analysis* 4, no. 3 (June 1980): 107-11.

26. M. B. Naqvi, "Strategic Overview of the Iran-Iraq War," *Defence Journal* (Karachi, Pakistan) 6, no. 10 (1980): 11-20.

27. Stork, 4.

28. Claudia Wright, "Implications of the Iran-Iraq War," *Foreign Affairs* 59 (Winter 1980-1981): 279-80.

29. Phebe Marr, "Iraq: Sociopolitical Developments," *AEI Foreign Policy and Defense Review* 2 (1980): 33-36; Dawisha, "Opportunity," 143.

30. Dawisha, "Iraq and the Arab World: The Gulf War and After," *The World Today* 37, no. 5 (May 1981): 190; Alieu B. S. Taal, "Wars and Religion," *New Zealand International Review* 6 (March-April 1981): 30.

# CHAPTER 4

# The War—The Initial Stages

A senior Baath Party official told the magazine *The Middle East* in the late fall of 1980 that the war had been planned for some time. He said the war was Saddam Husayn's: Saddam had never accepted as final the 1975 Algiers Accords, and, therefore, the countdown for war could be said to have started with the signing of those Accords. Getting more specific, however, he stated:

> The actual decision to launch a *limited* [author's emphasis] war against Iran was taken in August 1979, just after Saddam Husayn had taken over power from President Hassan al-Bakr. The actual preparation was left to the Army command, but the timing was to be set by the Revolutionary Command Council.[1]

The Iraqis began in early September with forays into the Qasr-e Shirin area and the central border area near Mehran. Iranian opposition, probably only border guards or gendarmerie, did not seem too potent. Emboldened by these modest successes and judging the Iranian military too debilitated by two years of turmoil to offer much of a defense, the Iraqi leadership decided to send its units into Khuzistan, anticipating a welcome from Iranian Arabs and a rapid collapse of Iranian resistance.

The Iraqi advance into Khuzistan was apparently based on an old plan that had existed for over 30 years. Drafted in 1950 with extensive British assistance, this plan envisioned an Iraqi invasion designed to force Tehran to concede Iraqi claims over the Shatt-al-Arab and disputed border regions. The plan called for besieging rather than assaulting cities and strong points and foresaw Iraqi occupation of Khuzistan. This accomplished, Baghdad would conduct negotiations from a position of strength.[2] The plan reportedly had been updated over the years, no doubt to take into consideration the vastly improved Iranian military capability since the early 1950s.

But it took only 11 days of fighting for Baghdad to realize it had made a ghastly mistake. The Khuzistani Arabs had not rallied to Iraq's banner of Arabism, Iranian regulars and paramilitary units continued to fight (albeit in a disorganized manner), and the IIAF—contrary to Iraqi expectations—had begun a strategic bombing campaign aimed at the centerpiece of Iraq's economy, its oil industry. As one observer noted, the Iranians had shown themselves little concerned with materialistic considerations.[3] Iraq's reaction was to stop overall offensive operations, declare the war won, and begin to look for a face-saving way out. On 2 October, the Iraqi Armed Forces General Command stated:

> In view of the fact that our valiant armed forces have accomplished their basic objectives, their military activities will henceforth be limited to retaining the targets achieved.[4]

Two days later, the Iraqi Defense Minister emphasized more pointedly that military operations were subordinate to decisions made by civilian leaders. While he affirmed that Iraq would continue to fight until Iranian decisionmakers responded appropriately, he felt compelled to deny Iraqi forces had stopped their attack. Neatly couching his terms, he said Iraqi forces had reached their targets, *which had been designated to them by the political command*, adding "We do not want to reach Tehran."[5]

The Iraqi leadership had given up. The Iraqi military, for all its flaws, would not try to win. The remainder of the war would be a continuous saga of Iran pursuing one goal—expulsion of the invaders and political victory. Meanwhile Baghdad, forbidden by Tehran to wriggle off the hook, would:

1. Alternate between threats and offers of conciliation.
2. Periodically try to tighten the screws on Iran, making Iran hurt at little cost to Iraq.
3. Try to reduce strong points bypassed in its initial advance and try to eliminate stubborn Iranian salients.
4. Attempt to bleed isolated Iran by attempting to form defensive walls on which the Iranian military waves would hopefully break themselves.
5. Endeavor to outlast Iran at least cost in manpower to itself.

What Iraq would not do was face up to the fact that a military victory was the only way out of the impasse, a solution involving risky and costly offensives. The Iraqi leadership chose to forgo the offensive and tried instead, much like the United States against North Vietnam, to up the ante by making Iran hurt enough so that it would have no other choice but to negotiate.

Though we may never know the specifics of Iraqi decisionmaking, it appears that Saddam Husayn, seeking a way out of this impasse, would alternately direct the IQAF to hit a few strategic targets and then back off, hoping the incremental damage would convince Tehran to let him off the hook. Like Lyndon Johnson and Ho Chi Minh in the 1960s, Saddam Husayn and Ayatollah Khomeini were fighting two different wars. Until Iran's late summer 1982 invasion of Iraq, Husayn's was a limited one in which he voluntarily restricted himself in order to seek limited aims. Khomeini's was total in which Iran used all its available resources wherever and whenever it could, conserved them where necessary, but never lost sight of the objective—to destroy the Iraqi regime.

To Western observers, airpower was still the key to victory, but the IIAF by early October could not by itself win for Iran and the option of a victory through IQAF airpower was an option the Iraqi leadership would not try, even if they had a doctrine that saw airpower as decisive, which they apparently did not. Baghdad's objective was no longer victory but survival. Airpower would play only a limited role in the attainment of that objective.

# NOTES

1. "Too Hot to Handle," *The Middle East* 73 (November 1980):10-11.

2. Richard Halloran, "British, in 1950, Helped Map Iraqi Invasion of Iran," *NYT*, 16 October 1980, A15. The subject of this plan is also mentioned in Col J. J. Haggerty, "The Seeds of Qadisizah [sic]—The Iraqi-Iranian War," *Army Quarterly and Defence Journal* 111, no. 1 (January 1981): 40-41. Haggerty's reference is made without footnotes and since he is a British author writing in a British publication, his comments about the plan have a ring of credibility to them. However, the timing of his and Halloran's report and the striking similarity in phrasing between the two articles leads one to the suspicion Haggerty got his information directly from the *New York Times* rather than directly from British sources.

3. Barry Rubin, "Iraq's Attack on Iran May Mean Less Than the Reasons Behind It," *Journal of Commerce*, 2 December 1980, 4.

4. Iraqi Armed Forces General Command Announcement Number 57 (hereafter referred to as AFGC, followed by the number), *Daily Report, Middle East and Africa* (Washington, D.C.: Foreign Broadcast Information Service) (hereafter referred to as *FBIS-MEA-year-number*), vol. 5, no. 194, 3 October 1980. Baghdad radio broadcast in Arabic at 1738 GMT, 2 October 1980.

5. "Defense Minister Holds Conference on Military Operations," *FBIS-MEA-80-195*, Iraqi News Agency (INA) in Arabic at 2150 GMT, 4 October 1980.

# CHAPTER 5

# The Air War

The ebb and flow of the conflict rarely made sense to outside observers. On balance, the war has continued with little actual ground movement. Even the 1982 Iranian offensives involve only a matter of a few kilometers movement on a long, but shallow, front. This lack of significant movement, combined with the hyperbolic and apocalyptic style of the two contenders' daily "victory" claims, has tended to deaden the senses and makes an understanding of the air war very difficult.

This study will, therefore, disregard the chronology of claims and counterclaims and will instead attempt to analyze the air war through three general subject areas. The first subject area incorporates the relationship of air forces to national objectives—what is the primary use for the Iraqi and Iranian Air Forces? The second subject area is a discussion of the importance of attrition to the two air forces. The third subject area is a discussion of the general airpower doctrines used by both air forces, often unconsciously expressed more through their actions (or lack of same) than through any known publications. The link between air force roles, attrition, and national objectives will be covered in the final chapter.

## Deterrence—The Primary Role for Air Forces

Air Force Manual 1–1, *Functions and Basic Doctrine of the United States Air Force*, lists nine basic US Air Force operational missions: strategic aerospace offense, space operations, strategic aerospace defense, airlift, close air support, air interdiction, counterair operations, surveillance and reconnaissance, and special operations.[1] Eliminating space operations, the remaining eight categories are an adequate description of missions required for both the IQAF and IIAF. The manner in which the US Air Force and the IQAF/IIAF carry out these missions may be different in style, but the essence of the missions is the same in kind. The most important mission for all three air forces—US Air Force, IQAF, IIAF—is strategic offensive.

For instance, AFM 1–1 states:

> Strategic aerospace offensive forces serve primarily as a deterrent to nuclear war. A vital part of deterrence is the credibility communicated by political will and forces in being. To preserve an attack capability, these forces must be able to survive an enemy attack and make successful retaliatory strikes.[2]

41

Nuclear war is not yet a concern of most Third World states, but strategic war is. Substituting "strategic" for "nuclear" in the above statement, we have the primary *raison d' être* for non-Israeli Middle East air forces. The primary role of both the IQAF and the IIAF is strategic deterrence. One glance at a map of the area shows why. The lynchpin of their economies is oil, and the great bulk of both countries' oil fields, refineries, and pumping stations are within 125 miles of their mutual borders. In a very real strategic sense, Iraq and Iran are in a "mutual (though not necessarily assured) destruction" situation. Their oil industries are very vulnerable to attack, and neither state can completely defend its oil industry from attack

But there is confusion here. In both countries, but especially in Iraq, the army is perceived as the decisive and most important military arm for two reasons. First, the concept that strategic bombing can destroy an enemy's capability and will to fight is not necessarily accepted, thus the army with its inherent ability to physically occupy enemy territory is perceived as the decisive military arm. Thus, air force missions are subordinated to army needs.* Second, the army has the internal political role of maintaining civil control, again through occupation. Because of this aspect of their mission, army commanders have more political, hence bureaucratic, clout. Therefore, in the relationship between the army and the air force, it is the army's needs which come first; the air force, for its part, must support these needs through its airlift, close air support, air interdiction, reconnaissance, and counterair capabilities. Western observers who saw this relationship were thus mystified when the IQAF especially did not seem to be supporting its ground forces. *The Economist* was puzzled by the lack of activity by "an air force whose main role was supposed to be close support of the ground forces."[3] An informed and insightful airpower professional, T. R. Milton, felt in January 1981 that there was "little evidence that either side is using its air forces for any objective purpose, whether air superiority, close air support, or planned interdiction."[4]

Such observations were correct if one assumes the primary mission of the respective air forces was to help their armies gain victory. But for the combatants, the primary benefit of their air forces was not the objectives that could be gained through the use of aircraft but the destruction that could be avoided through the deterrent posed by the possession of aircraft.

To help better clarify the use of airpower by Iraq and Iran, a review of some basic US ideas about airpower seems appropriate. AFM 1–1 again:

> The medium of aerospace provides an environment that allows unlimited horizontal and vertical movement for warfare systems. The freedom of operation permitted in aerospace allows our forces to exploit the characteristics of range, speed, and maneuverability. These characteristics enable the direct application of power against all elements of an enemy's military resources to a degree not possible by other forces.[5]

---

*Unfortunately for the countries involved, coordination between armies and air forces is lacking, and the potential for an air-ground team remains just that—a potential.

No disagreement here. But the aerospace environment is not solely owned by one side—the enemy can exploit range, speed, and maneuverability to put direct application of power against friendly resources. To continue with AFM 1–1:

> Aerospace power offers . . . flexibility, readiness, and responsiveness. It also offers presence, destructiveness, survivability, and mobility. . . . The concentration in time and space and the shock effect of the destruction that can be achieved by aerospace forces is without equal. Properly employed, aerospace forces are capable of selective or widespread destruction of any enemy forces and other assets.[6]

Again, little disagreement. Air forces do offer the aforementioned. But above all, they offer destruction and punishment, and here is where conceptions about airpower diverge.

For most Western observers, the air war between Iran and Iraq is generally a tactical air war, fought with tactical aircraft—F-4s, F-5s, Sukhois, and MiG-23s—delivering conventional ordnance. The respective combatants are organized as tactical air forces. The International Institute for Strategic Studies tends to regard nuclear capability as the characteristic distinguishing strategic from tactical forces. Doing so, it credits only the United States, Soviet Union, Britain, France, and China with strategic forces. Middle Eastern air forces are listed as if they are strictly tactical, having a variety of interceptor and ground attack squadrons. Parenthetically, Iraq additionally has two bomber squadrons.[7] *Aviation Week* noted on 6 October 1980 that airstrikes were at a level well below the limit of both sides' ability, but mistakenly felt that their "tactical airpower is being used to support the primary offensive and defensive efforts on the ground."[8] Thus, Western observers, thinking of Iran's and Iraq's air forces as purely tactical, would find "the lack of sustained application of Iraq's [in this case] airpower is one of the more puzzling aspects of the war."[9]

But it is less puzzling if one views the respective air forces in a strategic context. Both sides have strategic assets which they do not want destroyed, that is oil. But their oil cannot be defended adequately since it lies so close to the enemy and since it is a very soft target—refineries and storage areas can be heavily damaged by strafing, and tanker captains are loath to risk their ships if there is a serious prospect they may be attacked. Since neither side can defend its strategic assets, both must deter the other from striking them. Then, following very neatly our own description of strategic offensive forces, both the IQAF and the IIAF serve primarily as a deterrent to the other's ability to strike at strategic targets. Since a vital part of deterrence is credibility communicated by political will and forces inbeing, both sides must make the other aware that it has the forces (here the long-range striking forces—the air forces) capable of inflicting serious strategic damage as well as the determination to use them. To preserve this capability, the air forces must be able to survive enemy attacks and to make successful retaliatory attacks.

In the recent past, Middle Eastern air forces have been used as deterrents. In the Arab-Israeli confrontation, the thing Israel did not want to see attacked or destroyed was its populace. In 1956, for instance, Egyptian Il-28s were a deterrent to an Israeli assault on Egypt. Israel would not join Britain and France without assurances from them that Israeli cities would not be bombed. The rebuilt EAF was again a deterrent in 1967. Israel did not want to risk Egyptian bombing of Israeli cities. Israel's answer in 1967 was the same that Britain and France devised and implemented in 1956—it destroyed the EAF, Egypt's deterrent. If deterrence is composed of forces inbeing plus the will to use them, Egyptian deterrence failed because its credibility was destroyed when its forces were destroyed.

Egypt's vital strategic asset, the thing it did not want to see destroyed, was its army. Destruction of Egypt's deterrent, its air force, in 1956 and 1967 led to the destruction of the Egyptian army in both cases. Egypt's answer in 1973 was different from that of Israel in 1967. The EAF could not destroy Israel's deterrent, the IAF, but an integrated ground-based air defense system could (hopefully) neutralize it while the EAF protected rear areas from attack. Israeli deterrence failed in 1973 because Egypt decided its credibility could be lessened through ground-based air defense which would eviscerate its forces—the IAF.

The Iran-Iraq war is the first Middle East war between the "haves" of the region. People and armies, to be sure, are important, but the vital strategic asset for both sides, the resource both did not want to see destroyed, was the oil industry. One could make the case that for Iran's revolutionary leaders, their most vital asset was their revolution. But as they had proved to themselves that the shah's military could not destroy the psychic force of their revolution, they felt the same would be true for the Iraqi military. Thus their vital strategic asset, as it was for Iraq and as it was for the shah, was the material fuel for the revolution, the income derived from oil. In the Iran-Iraq context, the IIAF was Iran's deterrent to Iraqi attack. But Iranian deterrence failed. It failed because the credibility of its force—the IIAF—was suspect in Iraqi eyes. Without force, Iranian deterrence lacked persuasiveness to Iraqi decisionmakers.

Not that Baghdad had any doubt about Tehran's intentions or will. Iran's Abadan refinery, the largest in the world, lies right on the Shatt-al-Arab where it is extremely vulnerable to any type of military action. In 1972, Iran warned Iraq that any attack on Abadan would trigger massive air attacks against Iraqi oil fields at Kirkuk and Mosul.[10] The Tehran daily *Keyhan* warned on 25 August 1980 that "an air attack by Iraq will be met with . . . the destruction of Iraq's sensitive and strategic military positions."[11] But in Iraqi eyes, the credibility of that threat was weak. As previously mentioned, Baghdad assessed in late 1980 that Iranian military capability, especially the IIAF, was weak and probably figured any retaliatory strikes could be easily handled by what looked to be a formidable—though untested—network of SA-2s, SA-3s, and interceptors.

Given the disjointed *command and control arrangements* in the IIAF in late September 1980, it is likely that Iran would have retaliated for Iraq's invasion by striking Iraqi oil facilities whether or not Iraq struck Iranian oil facilities. But in initial ground movements on 23 September, Iraqi artillery rounds began hitting the Abadan refinery. Iraq then responded on the next day with strikes on oil facilities at Bandar-e Khomeini and Kharg Island. The IIAF continued with strikes on Mosul, Kirkuk, and Basra.

Neither Iranian nor Iraqi attacks on strategic targets were heavy or sustained enough to cause total destruction, but both were enough to cause severe damage and inflict punishment. Up to 30 percent of Iraqi oil facilities were estimated damaged. Iraqi oil loading facilities at the head of the Gulf were so damaged that they would take two years to repair or to replace.[12] As a result of this damage, Iraq was forced on 26 September to halt oil exports.[13] IIAF airstrikes, however, were not uniformly successful. One witness noted initial strikes on a Basra petrochemical complex missed the main plant and hit support facilities instead.[14] And F-4s trying to hit an oil refinery south of Baghdad missed the refinery by three-quarters of a mile.[15] But IIAF attacks on strategic targets were immediate, fairly large scale, and continued for several weeks. It is entirely probable that had the IIAF response early in the war been less massive or intense and had it not continued daily despite its losses, then the Iraqi leadership would have directed the IQAF to destroy the Iranian oil industry. (Their capability may have been lacking, but they would have been directed to make the attempt.) As it was, the IIAF response restored the credibility of the Iranian deterrent, and the attacks on strategic targets became part of a retaliatory cycle. The strikes on oil facilities were not irrational; they were not designed so much as a means of destroying the facilities in order to reduce the enemy's ability to fight as they were merely a means of punishing the enemy, of persuading him to cease hitting friendly oil targets.

Spokesmen for both sides were explicit in stating the reasons for the attacks on strategic targets. Iranian Defense Minister Fakuri on 23 September noted that the IIAF first hit airfields and then embarked on retaliatory attacks on strategic positions.[16] The Iraqi Defense Minister two days later referred to Iraqi strategic strikes also as retaliation and stated that if Iran bombed a civilian area or oil facilities, Iraq would do likewise. He blamed Iran for starting the strategic bombing phase, an act which forced Iraq to retaliate, thus escalating the war.[17] The strategic exchange took on the aspect of a blood feud with both sides retaliating, expecting the other to be the first to back off. On 6 October, an Iraqi Armed Forces General Command communiqué stated that IQAF bombing of Tehran on that day had been done "to make Tehran understand it should not hit civilian targets."[18] Retaliation and punishment were still the byword in December when Iranian officials explained that stepped-up IIAF operations against oil targets were in retaliation for IQAF raids on Iranian oil installations,[19] and Tehran radio's Arabic service noted that the Iranian effort to destroy Iraq's oil exporting terminal at the head of the Gulf was strictly for punishment, "dealing . . . an economic blow to the Iraqi regime."[20]

But even though strategic deterrence had so conspicuously failed in the fall of 1980, it was still a major concern for both countries' futures. Both had shown the other they had the will and the ability to inflict punishment, if not totally destroy each other's prized assets. But both had suffered severe losses while establishing that credibility. Iraq claimed to have downed 67 attacking Iranian aircraft on 23 September alone.[21] But the IQAF had not escaped unscathed either. An Iraqi official told a Kuwaiti newspaper in early October that the IQAF had lost 17 percent of its forces, adding however that it retained its basic effectiveness.[22] Continued losses of this magnitude would eventually erode any credibility their deterrents would have. Therefore, airframes and crews had to be conserved to preserve a credible deterrent for the future.

Hence, it was not solely that aircraft were being lost or that supplies were limited that caused a reduction in airstrikes or activity, but it was also because the possession of these planes created a deterrent to the other side's use of his planes. The planes could not objectively win the conflict, but they could inflict punishment *only*, however, so long as they existed. Using them to inflict higher levels of punishment, and losing them in the attempt, would only invite future retaliatory attacks for which there would be only a weak, if not nonexistent, response. Thus, it was not surprising when Saddam Husayn told the Iraqi National Assembly on 4 November that he would not allow the Western media to force him to use up his air force.

> We will not use our air force. We will keep it. Two years hence our air force will still be in a position to pound Bani-Sadr and his collaborators.[23]

## Performance—The IQAF and IIAF in Strategic Strikes

We have a problem evaluating the performance of both air forces in the strategic role since the goal of both seemed to be to induce the other to accept a mutual cessation of strategic attacks. It is difficult to use bombing accuracy as a measure, since it varied so. We already noted the IIAF had early in the war missed targets at Basra and Baghdad quite badly, but the IQAF raid on Tehran on the first day of the war was hardly an example to follow as it resulted in only light damage and two Iranians killed.[24] Despite a number of IQAF attacks, local residents at Tabriz reported the city unscathed in late September, and an attempt in October to bomb the Tabriz refinery was reported to have missed that fairly large and obvious target entirely.[25] On other occasions, attacking aircraft were very accurate. In early October, Western observers noted direct hits on the key Dawrah power plant at Baghdad, and IIAF attack aircraft caused considerable damage to oil pumping facilities in Kirkuk and a cement plant at Mosul.[26]

Effectiveness, however, can be used as a measure. Neither air force caused enough damage to the enemy to force him out of the war, but both did cause enough to force him to reduce his punishment attacks. IIAF attacks around Kirkuk caused Iraq to declare force majeure on 27 September and cease pumping oil through its pipelines which ran through Syria and Turkey to the Mediterranean.[27] These pipelines were not reopened until 21 November.[28] Kharg Island, Iran's major oil exporting terminal, had been closed at the start of the war, but it, too, was able to reopen on 22 November.[29] By that time, both Tehran and Baghdad knew each other had the capability to inflict more punishment on oil, but both had by then been deterred from continuing. From that time on, attacks on oil appeared to be ritualistic attempts to signal displeasure.

Renewed IIAF raids around Kirkuk, causing fires in storage tanks but not heavy enough to cause a cessation of the oil flow, were answered by Iraqi strikes at a petrochemical plant under construction at Bandar-e Khomeini. The plant had already been shut down when its Japanese workers had been pulled out, so the Iraqi attacks caused only more damage but did not significantly affect Iran's oil lifeline. Iran's late November "destruction" of Iraq's offshore oil loading platforms at Mina al-Bakr and Khor al-Amaya was answered by a resumption of IQAF raids on Kharg Island and Bandar-e Khomeini. But the destruction of the platforms was more or less a payback for the "destruction" of the Abadan refinery, and the retaliatory raids on Kharg caused little damage and scared off few tankers.[30]

So airstrikes on strategic targets by the two air forces were effective in restoring a situation of mutual deterrence but were not effective in forcing a decision. Why? One reason is they both used too few aircraft in their strikes. Observers never saw more than six aircraft in a single attack.[31] Only three IQAF aircraft hit Tehran in the opening attacks; only two IIAF planes were noted the next day in an attack on Baghdad; in another IIAF attack on Baghdad, two planes bombed while two covered for them.[32] By contrast, Israel in 1967 used 120 aircraft in its attacks on the Egyptian Air Force. Three waves of 40 planes each struck at Egyptian bases; then, refueled and rearmed, came back for a second attack for a total of 240 attack sorties.[33] The Israeli strategic attacks hit like a load of bricks, the Iranian and Iraqi attacks like pebbles.

Both sides also appeared to have a problem with unexploded ordnance.[34] The unexploded munitions problem may have been caused by both pilots and load crews. The pilots may have delivered their weapons well outside optimum parameters, but many of the weapons dropped on Iraqi targets, for instance, did not explode because they had been improperly fused and primed.[35] Part of the IIAF problem stemmed from the fact that load crews during the days of the shah had to be as politically reliable as the aircrews and were thus thoroughly checked out by the shah's internal security organization. After the revolution, anyone so thoroughly checked out and trusted by the shah's regime was immediately suspect under the revolutionary regime.

In all, the IIAF probably achieved better results than the IQAF. Despite its organizational problems, the IIAF carried Iran's fight to Iraq in the crucial early days of the war and, in doing so, let Baghdad know it could not expect an inexpensive victory. Overall, the IIAF hit harder than the IQAF. They seemed to put more effort into their offensive operations, and they probably caused more damage—especially in the northern oil areas around Kirkuk. US-trained Iranian aircrews seemed more aggressive and more willing to take risks than their Iraqi counterparts. IIAF aircraft were certainly better. The F-4 especially could carry a heavier ordnance load to longer ranges than could any IQAF planes. The IQAF was especially displeased with the capabilities of the MiG-23s. They had hoped to use these aircraft on strategic targets well inside Iran, but range and load problems severely limited their use.[36] Although little real damage was done in the raid, it served as a kind of "tap on the shoulder" to Baghdad, showing that nothing in Iraq was out of IIAF range.

## The Vital Importance of Attrition

An air force in this region must deter enemies from attacking strategic assets, so it must remain credible to remain a deterrent. Since credibility is a function of both will and forces inbeing, then air forces must be kept inbeing. They must be kept inbeing by being able to survive an enemy attack. This can be done by hardening the airfield, sheltering the aircraft, and having a robust air defense network. They can also be survivable if they are safehavened, as was the case with the Egyptian Air Force in 1956[37] and the IQAF in 1980.[38] But surviving enemy attacks is only part of the equation; an air force must survive its own attacks. There is a perceptual critical mass, a number of airframes and aircrews, below which the credibility of a deterrent evaporates. Enemy attacks reduce the size of the deterrent somewhat, but in this particular war the most severe losses for both sides seem to have occurred during offensive operations. The more the IQAF or IIAF presses the attack, the more planes and crews they lose through enemy responses, accident, or sheer usage, and the closer they fall toward that critical mass below which they do not want to drop. How is that critical mass defined? Is it an objective number, a subjective feel, or a perception of enemy perceptions? The answer is not readily apparent. Perhaps it does not even come under conscious consideration by IQAF and IIAF planners, but *it is there*!

One thing that makes the attrition problem all the more acute is the fact that Iran and Iraq, like most Third World countries, are, in essence, clients, suppliants of those industrialized states that produce aircraft. Leaders in nations whose defense industries produce aircraft know they have a more or less steady supply of replacement aircraft. No matter how long the production lead time, both Soviet and Western military planners know there will be a replacement for MiGs and F-16s lost in combat. On a smaller scale, while Argentine Air Force leaders must be uneasy about replacements for Mirages and A-4s lost in the Falklands, they know there will be replacements for Pucará aircraft lost to British gunners because the Pucará is produced in Argentina. In prior Middle Eastern wars, Israeli decisionmakers knew that links with the United States were so strong that replacement aircraft would be forthcoming should Israel really need them. Hence, Israel knew it had replacements even if they were not built by Israeli industry.

In these three cases, military and political decisionmakers have a much higher threshold of attrition pain than do those decisionmakers in a state that has neither industry nor reliable industrial friends. Military objectives can be pursued with more determination, and a higher level of airframe (but not necessarily aircrew) losses can be sustained by a state that has an ability to gain replacements. Even if that ability is only a perceived one in the minds of decisionmakers, they will act on the basis of their perceptions. A more determined use of aircraft may indeed lead to higher attrition, but it may also lead to a quick resolution of the conflict and, hence, lower long-term attrition, especially if one side in the conflict has a lower threshold of attrition pain.

Those who cannot count upon a dependable supply of replacements must always feel uneasy about committing their stock of airframes to combat. One way to reduce that unease is to stockpile as much equipment as possible in the hope that future conflicts will be limited sufficiently so that existing stockpiles will suffice. The shah had noted that Israel, heavily armed as it was, had needed a massive US airlift of arms during the 1973 war to continue the fight on Israeli terms. He, therefore, sought to purchase as much equipment as quickly as possible in order to reduce Iran's dependence on arms suppliers should a shooting war ever break out. He also bought a formidable strategic airlift capacity—707s and 747s—to further reduce Iranian dependence on arms suppliers. Iran, he planned, would not have to depend on a sole source of weaponry; Iran would possess a huge stockpile of equipment to fight, including transport aircraft to deliver arms purchased from foreign sellers or armament manufacturers.[39] Iraq's leadership saw the problem in a similar light. Saddam Husayn in a 1975 speech stated: "We believe that no country with serious problems which relies on importing its weapons can claim to be absolutely independent."[40] Consequently, Iraq, too, had built up a strategic airlift fleet, possessing 12 Il-76/Candid transports in 1980.

By 1980, both countries had a large amount of equipment, but neither had a secure, large-scale source of resupply. Unlike Israel or Egypt and Syria in 1973, Iran and Iraq in 1980 had no friends. Iran, holding American diplomats prisoner, was an international pariah. Iraq had over the years alienated its major supplier, the USSR, and Moscow had the opportunity in 1980-81 to take the high road of "neutrality," withholding major deliveries from Baghdad and teaching the Iraqis a lesson about the limits a supplier can impose upon a buyer.[41] Iraq could and did turn to other Western suppliers, like the French, but the Iraqi military had enough problems conducting a war without introducing new systems that would only further tax its logistics base.

So the essential attrition problem remained. Both sides were losing aircraft and inexorably reducing their strategic deterrents. Both sought out other supplies and suppliers to ameliorate the problem, but neither could depend upon having a secure enough source to ensure a continuing balance between losses and replacements. The need to reduce their losses thus led both sides to limit the use of their aircraft in high-threat environments.

The number and intensity of attacks on strategic (oil and industrial) targets began to decline about 8 October, having fairly well petered out as a daily occurrence by the end of the month. Through November and December, IIAF aircraft kept up random attacks on Iraqi oil targets, chiefly in the north around Mosul and Kirkuk. IQAF strategic attacks followed a similar pattern, slacking off to almost none by 1

November. Deep strikes into the Tehran area were discontinued after 16 October. Tu-22s had struck at Mehrabad Airport on the first day of the war and at a refinery and industrial area in the southern section of the city on three other occasions through 16 October. Perhaps feeling it had made clear its capability to strike Iran's capitol (even though its strikes caused no major dislocation), Baghdad decided to cut its bomber losses by restricting further attacks to targets closer to the border where IQAF aircraft would be exposed to defenses for a smaller period of time. Random airstrikes on Iran's vital oil loading facility at Kharg Island continued through April. They had no lasting effect on Iranian oil exports since they appeared to be similar to the IIAF's raids into northern Iraq—small scale, hit-and-run efforts seemingly designed to advertise a capability and to inflict some measure of punishment while limiting exposure to defenses and thereby holding down attrition. The increased numbers of interdiction attacks launched by both air forces after the first few weeks of the war was a reflection of both doctrinal and attrition needs. The incredible Iranian Joint General Staff Announcement Number 82 on 28 September stated that:

> Now that IIAF pilots have, and will destroy military targets [sic] inside Iraq, they have commenced their severe counterattack on enemy units which have infiltrated our dear country.[42]

This statement was both a reflection of having run through most of the preplanned missions left over from prerevolutionary days and a recognition that continuance of those kinds of missions into high-threat areas would reduce the IIAF to impotence. Accordingly, both sides began to seek out interdiction-type targets in less heavily defended areas.

All attrition is not, however, the same. Dr Williamson Murray, a former research associate at the Air University's Airpower Research Institute, in his study of Luftwaffe operations during World War II postulated three different types of attrition—offensive, response, and imposed. *Offensive attrition* are those calculated losses caused by one's own initiative that one is willing to suffer in an effort to achieve a gain through the offensive use of airpower. Offensive attrition is that which the Israeli Air Force had to accept in 1973 when it took high losses in its effort to knock out Syrian SA-6s on the Golan front.[43] The IIAF suffered offensive attrition when it struck back hard at Iraqi strategic targets on 23 September 1980, losing a good number of aircraft (67 by Iraq's probably overoptimistic claim). IQAF losses during attacks in Tehran, including at least two Tu-22s in October,[44] were similarly caused by Iraqi initiative.

Conversely, *response attrition* is that caused by enemy initiative, the losses you suffer by either being destroyed on the ground or by defending yourself from enemy attack. The Egyptian Air Force losses in 1956 and 1967 were classic examples of response attrition, though the EAF was given little opportunity to respond. In 1973, the EAF accepted a certain level of offensive attrition in its opening airstrikes into the Sinai but sought to reduce its response attrition through hardening of airfields and by restricting the EAF's defensive responsibilities while increasing those of ground-based air defense. Neither the IIAF nor the IQAF suffered very much response attrition for several reasons—one, both had hardened air bases; two, neither air force mounted a sustained counterair offensive; three, Iraq especially tended to rely more on SAMs and AAA for defense; and four, neither really had to contend with enemy fighter sweeps or escort aircraft as part of strike packages.

Finally, *imposed attrition* is that which is forced upon you by the demands of the situation. As such, it is an outgrowth of both offensive and response attrition. But while one can avoid the first two types of attrition—by exercising no initiative in the first case or not contesting the issue in the second—imposed attrition cannot be avoided. When it became apparent to Egypt in 1973 that the Israeli Suez Canal crossing at Deversoir threatened the existence of the Egyptian Third Army and perhaps the entire Egyptian army, the EAF was thrown into the fray for the first time in a desperate attempt to salvage the situation. Most of the losses the EAF suffered occurred in this effort. But the EAF could do nothing else than to try to save the army, regardless of the long odds it faced. The attrition the EAF suffered was imposed on it; it could not be avoided.

Neither the IIAF nor the IQAF was ever really forced into such a position. The IIAF, especially, seemed to feel that the offensive attrition it suffered was high enough to cause the IQAF to back off on the pressure. The IQAF was not willing or was unable to bear the offensive attrition cost required to impose crushing losses on either the IIAF or Iran itself. The same was true of the IIAF. Attrition through offensive action was too high to sustain, so lower threat missions became the norm regardless of their minimal impact on the course of the war. For both air forces, and especially for the IQAF, the gains achievable through airpower outweighed the perceived loss of power that accompanied the attrition of their aircraft. Palpable losses that could not be quickly replaced weighed more on Iraqi and Iranian decisionmakers than did theoretical gains that might be achieved. Victory in the war, if it was to be achieved, would be gained by the army. The air force would assist the army if it did not cost too much in attrition of aircraft assets.

## Performance—The IQAF and IIAF in Strategic Defense

Although defenses inside Iran and Iraq inflicted enough attrition upon enemy air forces to cause the respective national leaderships to abandon strategic bombing as a major part of their war effort, the overall defensive performance on both sides was not particularly good. The early warning radar networks, in particular, seemed totally ineffective. Iraqi bombers were able to penetrate to Tehran on at least three occasions without meeting any IIAF opposition until *after* they had already delivered their ordnance. While IQAF flight planners could have used terrain masking to penetrate the mountainous areas along the border, their ability to fly undetected as far inland as Tehran, Shiraz, and Isfahan must have been, at least in part, a reflection of intelligence on Iranian radar capabilities obtained from Iranian exiles who cooperated with Baghdad.[45] Similarly, Iranian aircraft were able to strike targets inside Iraq, apparently unhindered by IQAF interceptors while en route to their targets. The Iraqi defensive problem was compounded, however, by geographic realities. Iraqi strategic targets all lay relatively close to the Iranian border where the topography is very mountainous. This allowed IIAF strike aircraft to fly low through Iranian mountain passes, popping out into Iraqi radar coverage only after having already crossed the border. IIAF run-ins to targets were often a matter of only a few minutes after border crossing.

The ability of the IIAF, flying low and fast, to arrive unhindered over Iraqi cities led some to conclude that the entire Iraqi defensive command and control structure had either collapsed or was extremely incompetent.[46] While the Iraqi defensive system undoubtedly had severe shortcomings, this appears to be too harsh a judgment. French reporters in Baghdad routinely heard warnings of impending attacks well before Iranian aircraft appeared over the city.[47] It appears a major reason Iranian aircraft were able to get to their target relatively unmolested was the Iraqi defensive setup. It appeared that the Iraqis had made those areas which were well equipped with air defense weapons into virtual free-fire zones. Thus, any aircraft over areas like Baghdad, Basra, and possibly Kirkuk were assumed to be hostile and free game for Iraqi gunners. The IQAF would not attempt an intercept in these areas due to the inability of Iraqi ground air defenses to discriminate between friend or foe. The IQAF apparently, therefore, flew combat air patrols (CAPs) over certain areas that did not have ground-based air defenses and would only intercept Iranian penetrators when the Iranians came inside the IQAF CAP area. While this system limited IQAF flexibility to cope with IIAF intruders and allowed IIAF pilots to face only one defensive problem at a time, the Iraqis were probably sensible to adopt it. In their enthusiasm, Iraqi gunners reportedly downed one of their own Il-76 transports over Baghdad on the first day of the war.[48]

Iraq's defensive problems were also compounded by the high-expenditure rate of SAMs and AAA rounds. Western observers in Baghdad and Basra noted SAMs and artillery rounds all over the sky during Iranian raids early in the war, raids that probably comprised two to, at most, four aircraft.[49] A British reporter who arrived in Baghdad two weeks into the war noted, "The rain of spent shells even interrupted tennis on the British Embassy lawn."[50] The resultant rapid depletion of ammunition stocks that Iraq's suppliers were not refilling obviously became a complicating factor for Iraqi air defense planners.

From the Iraqi perspective, another problem was the ability of Iranian pilots to avoid Iraqi SA-2s and SA-3s. Many IIAF aircrews were able to turn inside Iraqi surface-to-air missiles by using tactics taught them by US Air Force instructors.[51] One Iraqi response was to withdraw some of their limited number of SA-6s from the front inside Iran and place them around strategic targets, thus leaving too few SA-6s to be very effective at either location.[52]

The Iranian strategic defensive setup was harder to determine. It appeared Iran depended more on fighters for defense than on SAMs if only because Iranian SAMs were in such a bad state of readiness. *Iranian combat reports* claimed about equal numbers of Iraqi losses caused by AAA and by Iranian fighters. While most of the AAA claims were near the battlefront, a number were also claimed in the Kharg Island-Büshehr area, indicating Iranian concern with the defense of this terminal. Most of the interception claims were in areas behind the front lines, indicating IIAF aircraft on airborne alert had been vectored to intercept Iraqi intruders. One of its most important roles appeared to be as an airborne early warning platform, detecting intruders with its AWG-9 radar and informing other aircraft who then tried for the interception.[53] F-14s apparently did not get too close to the fight for some time as it was not until March 1981 that *Iraqi dispatches* mentioned any F-14 encounters.

Iraqi leaders seemed very displeased with Iraqi defensive performances and seemed inclined to blame their Soviet-supplied equipment rather than acknowledge their own structural problems. Although undoubtedly Soviet equipment has its shortcomings, the relatively poor Iraqi performance cannot be totally laid at the feet of the Soviet Union. At any rate, the Iraqis began to seek out French equipment to supplement and/or replace the Soviet equipment with which they were displeased. Baghdad approached the French in late 1980 with requests to buy Crotale and Roland surface-to-air missile systems to augment their depleted Soviet SAM arsenal.[54] The Iraqis were also displeased with Soviet air-to-air missiles. Pakistani technicians were reported to have helped the Iraqis modify some MiG-21s to carry the French-made Magic air-to-air missile. The Iraqis claimed to have used a MiG-21 so equipped to down an F-14.[55] Additionally, in early 1981 the Iraqis received the first of their 1977 order of 36 Mirage F-1s.[56] This move to French equipment was due not only to real problems with Soviet equipment but also to politics and expedience. Politically, Baghdad wanted more than one arms supplier so Iraqi actions could not be as easily manipulated by a sole seller. And since the French seemed willing to sell to a combatant while the Soviets were not, the move appeared quite logical. New equipment, however, would not alter Iraq's geographical realities on the Iranian front nor would it improve Iraqi reaction time, as the Israelis were to demonstrate so dramatically when they destroyed Iraq's nuclear reactors at Tawaitha in June 1981.

## Doctrinal Approaches

Since for both Baghdad and Tehran the existence of an air force is essential in order to deter potential enemies from attempting to destroy strategic assets, then the attrition of that air force is of vital concern. But the use of those air forces as deterrents and the subsequent concern with the attrition of that deterrent are an outgrowth of basic doctrinal attitudes about the value and utility of airpower. While these attitudes can be stated or codified, the use to which both Iran and Iraq put their air forces display their operational attitudes, whether they be formulated in manuals and regulations or unconscious and unstated, but understood.

Iran and Iraq—and by extension most of the other Middle East states—seem to have fundamentally different ideas than does the US Air Force about the importance, utility, and role of air forces. US Air Force ideas have been codified in basic doctrine that has evolved over a period of 60-odd years. And it *has* been an evolutionary process. At times, visionary ideas and thinkers have outpaced aviation technology; at others, technology has increased capabilities faster than the development of the ideas on how to best use the newer capabilities. In the evolution of US Air Force doctrine, the basic belief that "aerospace forces are unique and can be decisive in warfare,"[57] coupled with World War II experience, led US Air Force doctrine away from linking airpower with ground forces to a position where there was a measure of equality between air and ground forces. The air forces were to be independent of army control though their joint cooperation was a must. (FM 100-20, *Command and Employment of Air Power*, declared in 1943 that air superiority was a requirement for successful land operations.)[58] To repeat, for the US Air Force, it has been an evolutionary process. In the period preceding World War II, airpower thinkers developed concepts that were to be tried in the fire of that war. One of the results of that trial by fire was an independent US Air Force. It has since become an article of faith that airpower is the decisive element in war when the air war is conducted in a proper manner.[59]

The key to the development of US Air Force doctrine was its long-term growth in concert with emerging technology and an expanding experience base from which to draw lessons. Such has not been the case for the IQAF and IIAF. As previously noted, both air forces are fairly new creations in which near state-of-the-art aviation technology has been force-fed to a human resource base barely able to cope with the pressures of modernity.

Although the IQAF dates from the early 1930s, it remained almost fully under British control through 1955. The radical shift after 1958 to Soviet weapons brought in a new group of advisers, a different language, and different styles. This influence was subsequently modified over the next two decades by successive periods of close, then frosty, Moscow-Baghdad relations. By 1980, the IQAF possessed a mixture of Soviet, Czech, British, and French aircraft and had been influenced by British, Soviet, and Indian instructors. Furthermore, Iraqi airmen had only limited combat experience, and none of it was at a level of command which required coordination and operation of more than a small segment of the airpower spectrum. While IQAF leaders could study Arab experiences in wars since 1948, their own part in those wars had been quite limited. While their doctrine—as displayed through their actions in the war with Iran—seemed to offer lip service to the generally accepted tenets of airpower, one had the feeling that Iraqi leaders had no real faith in the efficacy of airpower. It seemed that the most important factors affecting the IQAF were not the capabilities of their aircraft nor the employment ideas of IQAF leaders, but rather the subordination of the air force to the needs of not only the army but also, and more important, the political command.[60]

The IIAF situation was at once both similar to and different from that of Iraq. The IIAF was a newer creation than the IQAF, receiving its first combat aircraft only in 1956. The 1970s was a period of explosive growth for the IIAF as the force structure, composed of first-rate American aircraft, increased rapidly. The need to find somehow the necessary manpower to operate the equipment was a pressing priority. (A 1976 study estimated that the IIAF would have to increase personnel levels by over 50 percent by 1981 to operate all the systems expected in the inventory by that date.)[61] But at least the aircraft, and hence the foreign assistance, all came from one source—the United States. By the end of the shah's era, the IIAF had no written doctrine, but the close US Air Force-IIAF ties over the preceding years had resulted in many IIAF officers internalizing aspects of US Air Force doctrine. According to a US Air Force officer intimately familiar with the command echelons of the Imperial Iranian Air Force, IIAF commanders, *to the extent they even recognized a need for doctrine*, tended to use ours.[62] IIAF planners, often schooled in US Air Force professional military education schools, attempted to correct this shortcoming by injecting doctrinal ideas into the "concept of operations" sections of contingency plans. As previously mentioned, the IIAF tried to gain a separate identity; but, like the IQAF, was never really free from close political control by national leaders more concerned with their own security than with national defense or institutional professionalism. Before 1978, the shah's influence was paramount; in 1980, the mullahs kept close rein on the IIAF lest it become a tool for opposition elements.

In 1980 and 1981, any doctrinal impulses held by either the IQAF or IIAF (about how best to prosecute the war) were definitely constrained by the political needs of the regimes in Baghdad and Tehran. IQAF and IIAF actions during the war, however, displayed their operational attitudes, and possibly their nascent doctrine, about the uses of airpower. The next sections of this study will examine how these two air forces approached the basic tactical airpower tasks, noting the divergence between their and our beliefs.

## Offensive Counterair Operations

"The first task of airpower is to gain and [to] maintain air superiority. Air superiority is essential to sustained air, ground, and sea operations."[63]

"Offensive counterair operations are conducted to seek out and destroy enemy forces that compete with us for air superiority. We must destroy the enemy's offensive counterair systems and support facilities . . . air superiority is essential."[64]

These statements describe the US Air Force beliefs about the primacy of air superiority, especially the primacy of the offensive counterair mission. It is patently obvious to most American airpower practitioners that all other military operations will suffer unacceptable hardships without air superiority being first attained. It is also equally obvious, but not so often expressed, that if ground operations, for example, can be carried out with a lack of air superiority, then there's less reason for exclusive US Air Force control of Air Force assets. These same factors also may be apparent to Iraqi and Iranian air force leaders, but they are not so readily obvious to their respective national military and political chiefs.

## The Iraqi Attack

The Iraqis had learned one airpower lesson from previous Middle Eastern wars—the necessity of the first strike. The first strike had been decisive in 1956 and 1967. In 1973, the first strike had not been decisive in achieving air superiority, but it had helped the Arab attack gain enough momentum to gain key ground, especially on the Suez front. In 1980, the Iraqis were in an ambiguous situation. Their assessment of Iranian military weakness indicated they had a window of opportunity through which they could launch a successful attack. But they had little real faith in their equipment. Like the Egyptians in 1973,[65] the Iraqis knew their Soviet-supplied aircraft were no match for Iran's US-supplied aircraft. Their planes had short ranges, making deep strikes difficult and giving Iran in-country sanctuaries; they had mediocre avionics; and they had no capacity to carry advanced munitions. Atop all this, Iranian pilots had, quoting Saddam Husayn, "received training from the most experienced Americans."[66] The Iraqi decision to launch the attack, therefore, had to rest on the assessment that despite the IQAF's equipment shortcomings, it could succeed against a revolution-wracked IIAF.

But success for Iraq, like Egypt in 1973, did not necessarily mean air superiority. AFM 2-1, *Tactical Air Operations—Counter-Air, Close Air Support, and Air Interdiction*, states control of the air may vary along a spectrum ranging from total friendly control to total enemy control.[67] It also states that offensive action is necessary to gain friendly control as defensive action surrenders initiative to the enemy.[68] The Iraqis, like the Egyptians, saw it differently. Rather than strive for total air superiority, they would be content with localized air control. Rather than seek out and destroy the enemy air force, they would surrender the initiative but try to destroy the enemy whenever he approached the areas they wanted to control. An Iraqi military source was reported to have said in late September 1980 that ground air defense is the best means of reducing and destroying the IIAF.[69]

Why, then, the 22 September attacks on Iranian air bases? Iraqi leaders, agreeing with AFM 2–1, felt that employment of their airpower could have a political effect. It would demonstrate national resolve (tell Tehran that Iraq meant business) and could serve as a deterrent to further escalation of the conflict.[70] While Iranian spokesmen and Western observers characterized the Iraqi attack as an attempt to duplicate Israel's 1967 feat, the attack was much more in line with Egypt's initial airstrikes into the Sinai in 1973. Like the Egyptians in 1973, the Iraqis knew they had little chance to destroy the IIAF. Iranian aircraft were mostly held in hardened shelters, and several major airfields were either at the ragged edge of IQAF fighter capabilities or beyond it entirely. Iraq's 22 September counterair attacks were, therefore, to be like Egypt's 1973 attacks—hit-and-run affairs to disrupt potential IIAF reactions to Iraqi ground forces that were preparing to invade early the following morning. If the attacks persuaded the Iranians not to fight, well and good; if they only hampered IIAF ability to interfere with Iraqi ground forces, then they were successful.

On the afternoon of 22 September 1980, the Iraqis expanded the border conflict. Iraqi aircraft, on apparent counterair missions, struck at 10 Iranian airfields, including Mehrabad Air Base at Tehran and bases at Shiraz, Būshehr, Dezfūl, Ahwaz, and Omidiyeh.[71] Damage was relatively light due to several possible factors including that IIAF aircraft were not parked in the open, the strike forces apparently attacked in only one wave with relatively light ordnance (due to aircraft capability and range problems), or that the Iraqis suffered from extremely poor prestrike intelligence. The Egyptians in 1973 had the benefit of Soviet satellites[72] and MiG-25 reconnaissance photos[73] of Israeli dispositions in the Sinai. With this information, they had been able to pinpoint their targets for their first strike. Iraq probably did not have this advantage since in 1980 relations between Baghdad and Moscow had been strained for over two years.

The airstrike on Mehrabad displayed the Iraqi problems. While making a shallow right-hand turn to correct this, they released their bombs (a number of which did not explode), thus spraying them all over the area with some bombs landing outside the base perimeter. The resultant pattern made it difficult for the Iranians to determine the Blinders' actual targets. Two bombs caused the only damage. One hit a loaded KC-707 tanker and the other hit a ramp in front of Iran Aircraft Industries where an F-4 awaiting overhaul was destroyed. Bombs that hit the runways caused very shallow craters that were easily repaired. Rows of unprotected civil and military transports remained unscathed. What appeared to be poor IQAF airmanship and poor target intelligence combined to produce little significant damage to the IIAF. Iraqi intelligence about en route defenses, however, appeared adequate since the Blinder attack came as a complete surprise, and it was unopposed.

In follow-on attacks, fewer bases were hit. On the 23d, four airfields were attacked, including Tabriz and Büshehr twice. On the 24th, six were attacked—Tabriz twice, Dezful twice, and Shahrokhi, Kermanshah, Ahwaz, and Sanandaj once each respectively. By the third day of the war, Iraqi counterair strikes were limited to a few bases close to the border from which the IIAF was launching retaliatory raids.[74] The only IIAF base successfully neutralized was at Dezful. Probably because it was closest to Iraq, it was hit more often than others; on the 23d, damage was great enough to prevent returning IIAF fighters from landing.[75] It was neutralized eventually when Iraqi ground forces closed in on Dezful. After the first week of the war, IQAF counterair strikes apparently became much more random affairs. Since air superiority was viewed as desirable but not essential, Iraqi decisionmakers felt no need to continue an offensive counterair campaign even though the IIAF had not been neutralized. By then, too, Iraqi leaders were facing another problem—IIAF strikes against strategic targets inside Iraq.

The Iraqi offensive counterair effort lasted less than a week and can be judged a total failure. The damage the IQAF inflicted on the IIAF was minimal and did not severely damage IIAF retaliatory capabilities. But the Iraqis saw their air force primarily as a deterrent force—official Iraqi announcements, in fact, referred to the 22 September attacks as "a deterrent blow."[76] While exact IQAF losses in the first week are not known, they were high enough to convince the Iraqis that IQAF airframes could be more productively used. The counterair mission would be carried out through defensive measures.

## The Iranian Response

The original Iranian approach to the air superiority question was very similar to the one espoused by the US Air Force. Contingency plans, drafted before the revolution, envisaged IIAF actions in an air war with Iraq starting with a strong counterair effort. The initial IIAF reaction followed the existing plans as IIAF aircraft struck back at two Iraqi air bases on 22 September.[77] But the plans envisage attacks on Iraqi airfields to be undertaken by large strike packages with F-14s providing top cover, F-4s providing defense suppression, and F-4 and F-5 bombers carrying both cratering and area-denial munitions. Further exacerbating the situation for the attackers was the fact that they lacked good current intelligence about target defenses and did not have defense suppression support; as a result, the IIAF suffered heavily. IIAF offensive counterair missions continued only through the fourth day of the war, then stopped.

The IIAF command element in Tehran, hampered as it was by civilian suspicion and by the loss of most of its prerevolutionary leadership, still seemed to sense quite quickly that its counterair effort was counterproductive. As it sought to regain operational control (discussed in a future section) from the air bases which were operating autonomously, they began to issue frag orders directing attacks on Iraqi strategic targets. In apparently classic statements of bravado that sought to mask severe difficulties, the joint chiefs in Tehran announced on 26 September that the IIAF had control of Iranian airspace.[78] Then on 28 September, they announced that the IIAF would turn its attention to the support of the Iranian army, having already destroyed all Iraqi military targets.[79] In reality, IQAF aircraft could still penetrate Iranian airspace nearly at will, and IIAF aircraft would still strike into Iraq. IIAF aircraft would not, however, continue a counterair effort. The primary mission of the IIAF would not be the destruction or neutralization of enemy air; the IIAF moved to its deterrent role. The IIAF would now punish Iraqi strategic targets in order to dissuade the Iraqis from bombing Iranian targets.

The counterair mission had been tried by both sides, then abandoned. Neither put a full weight of effort into it and both achieved what one could have expected—next to nothing. From the doctrinal point of view, the reasons for the counterair fiasco appear different for the two air forces. The IQAF appears not to believe in offensive counterair. It made a half-hearted, fill-in-the-square attempt at it. The IQAF apparently believed in and preferred attrition inflicted through defensive counterair and ground-based air defense as the way to reduce enemy air capabilities. In contrast, the IIAF seemed , to believe in the need for offensive counterair but found that pilot shortages and heavy losses forced it to abandon this mission. If a depleted IIAF was to have an effect on the war, it would have to be in another role—and that role, at first, was to inflict punishing strategic strikes.

## Support for Ground Forces—Close Air Support/Interdiction

After the IQAF and IIAF both tackled their strategic missions, they then had to address their primary tactical mission—support for ground forces. Since, in both Iran and Iraq, the army is the most important military arm, air force support for the ground forces is an important task, and the approach to it taken by the IIAF and IQAF differs little from US Air Force doctrine, with one major exception. While both sides talk about close air support (CAS) for their ground forces, in reality neither air force really carried out the CAS role except in extremely dire situations. One of the lessons the Iraqis had drawn from the 1973 war was that CAS was likely to be too costly in terms of attrition for the results gained. They had noted the losses suffered by the Israeli Air Force on the Suez front when trying to perform the CAS role in the teeth of the integrated Egyptian air defense system. They had also suffered severe losses of their own, tangling with the Israeli Air Force over the Golan Heights as they tried to support Iraqi armored units being chewed up on the ground.

So in 1980, the IQAF did not perform the CAS role in support of Iraqi army units moving into Iran. The lack of IQAF activity near the front consistently surprised Western reporters up until the time they were forbidden to cover the battle area.[80] The IQAF seemed doctrinally to have attached a low priority to CAS. From a doctrinal standpoint, IQAF leaders seem to have decided, on the basis of the 1973 experience, that tactical aircraft could not survive the deadly air defenses active in the zone of ground forces confrontation. While this appeared true on the Suez front in 1973, the Khuzistan front in 1980–81 was certainly a less dangerous place. True, Iran possessed both Hawk and Rapier SAMs, but Iranian SAMs (unlike the case with Egyptian SA-6s on the Suez front) were not integrated with Iranian ground force units. Iranian AAA, on paper, looked potent with some 1,800 23-mm, 35-mm, 40-mm, 57-mm, and 85-mm towed AAA pieces and 100 ZSU 23-4 and ZSU 57-2 self-propelled guns.[81] But if the Iranian army was disorganized and weak enough for Iraqi leaders to have decided an invasion would cause its collapse, then the Iranian battlefield air defense system should have been suspect enough for the Iraqis to have at least tried to fly against it. Two possible reasons exist for the IQAF's apparent disinterest in CAS. First, Iraqi air-ground coordination may have been quite weak and the IQAF may have decided to forgo CAS rather than contend with trigger-happy Iraqi antiaircraft gunnery, as well as with whatever Iranian air defenses that might have existed. And second, the IQAF, over the years since 1973, doctrinally may have dropped CAS from a priority air force mission to one to be flown only in desperate circumstances.

The Iranians talked about CAS, both before and during the conflict, but they too flew very few CAS missions. But the missions the direct air support centers (DASCs) coordinated included very little true CAS. Iranian planners had decided that the Arab-Israeli and India-Pakistan wars had shown that CAS was likely to be too costly when flown in the face of a sophisticated air defense network. And, like the Iraqis, the Iranians had decided before the revolution that enemy possession of sophisticated air defense equipment implied enemy proficiency with that equipment; this assumption of proficiency was apparently never seriously tested. By 1980, the IIAF had developed a program of army support referred to as CAS, but that, in actuality, more resembled battlefield area interdiction (BAI). IIAF aircraft would be detailed through the DASCs to army units, but they would not strike close to the zone of confrontation between the armies. Instead, they would operate in enemy-held areas behind that zone, opposite their assigned army units. IIAF fighters thus did a lot of strafing and rocketing of targets of opportunity along the roads leading to the battle areas. While such attacks ranged as far into Iraq as the Al 'Amārah area on the Khuzistan front, they generally occurred near the border on the central front from Mehran to Qasr-e Shīrīn.[82]

Under these circumstances, both Iran and Iraq increasingly turned the CAS role over to helicopters. Attack helicopters were first reported on the battlefield in early October 1980 and soon became a regular feature in Iranian and Iraqi reports. Iranian Cobra helicopter gunships armed with tube-launched, optically-tracked, wire-guided (TOW) antitank missiles apparently had considerable success against Iraqi armored units that at times advanced without any air cover. A French reporter noted three Cobras taking turns attacking an Iraqi column near Abadan in mid-October 1980. The Cobras apparently faced no Iraqi antiaircraft fire.[83] By November, however, Iraqi use of ZSU-23-4 antiaircraft gun systems, as well as tank-mounted machine guns, began to take a toll of Iranian helicopters, particularly in flat areas of Khuzistan.[84]

The attack helicopter, though, was never driven from the skies, and the use of helicopters in CAS, close-in interdiction, and artillery-spotter roles continued throughout the war. While antiaircraft fire proved the most effective means for defense from attack helicopters, the IQAF succeeded several times in using fighters to down Iranian helicopters.[85] And on 24 April 1981, the Iranians reported air-to-air combat between helicopters stating Iranian helicopters "blew up two enemy helicopters during a dogfight."[86]

Although they neglected close air support, both the IQAF and IIAF flew a good number of interdiction sorties. Early in the war, the IQAF began striking at Iran's transportation infrastructure, hitting a number of bridges, railroads, and roads. IQAF fighters also struck at depots, troop positions, and armor and vehicle concentrations, but never seemed to strike at Iranian reinforcements moving toward the battle area. Iraqi interdiction efforts were at their highest levels during the first 45 days of the war, then tapered off. Except for increased numbers of interdiction sorties in mid-December 1980 and around the area of Iran's ill-fated Sūsangerd counterattack in January 1981, the IQAF interdiction effort wound down through the spring and summer of 1981 to random and periodic missions, generally in areas close to the battle areas.[87]

Although the IIAF continued a higher level of effort for a longer period of time, the IIAF interdiction effort generally paralleled that of the IQAF. Iranian interdiction sorties remained fairly constant through mid-January 1981 but declined thereafter. They picked up again in April and May but were carried out against only a few areas on a daily basis, whereas their effort in late 1980 had been more intensive and spread over a greater area both inside Iraq as well as near the battle areas.

IIAF interdiction aircraft struck most often along the roads inside Iraq in an area centered on Al 'Amarāh, Iraq—an area generally parallel to the Iranian border from Dezfūl to Abadan. IIAF aircraft struck at Iraqi garrisons inside Iraq—at apparently poorly protected depots, ammunition dumps, and vehicle concentrations—and against Iraqi units moving along the roads toward Iran. Early in the war, American reporters watched the IIAF, flying singly and in two-plane sorties, cause considerable havoc on Iraqi positions. On 30 September, 12 miles west of Ahwaz, they watched two F-4s destroy an Iraqi ammunition dump.[88] Much of the Iranian interdiction effort was similar to that of the Iraqis—aircraft on armed reconnaissance struck at targets of opportunity. An American reporter, traveling in a car along the Iraqi side of the Shatt-al-Arab, became a target when an IIAF F-4 flying along the road at 100 feet noted his taxi. The pilot banked the aircraft into a 360-degree turn and attempted to bomb the taxi on the second pass.[89]

Overall, the interdiction effort, by both air forces, seemed to be characterized by a lot of armed reconnaissance and strafing, with somewhat less effort put into hitting preplanned targets. From the targets they hit and the description given by their *public claims*, it seems the Iraqis did most of their interdiction targeting on the basis of maps rather than other target materials. As noted earlier, the Iraqis probably had received very limited prewar target information from the Soviets and apparently received none during the war. Iraqi tactical reconnaissance seemed almost nonexistent, so updated information about Iranian targets had to come primarily from debriefings of strike pilots. Most of the transient-type targets appeared to have been targets of opportunity struck by aircraft or armed reconnaissance missions. When the IQAF attacked targets of opportunity, the results were sometimes spectacular. For instance, in early October a French correspondent reported that an Iraqi aircraft had hit a rail-switching center between Khorramshahr and Bandar-e Khomeini. The plane's rockets blew up an entire string of liquified petroleum gas (LPG) cars.[90]

The IIAF, by contrast, seemed to have better target intelligence. Contingency target folders, built before the revolution, had target materials derived from RF-4E photoreconnaissance sorties carried out over Iraq at least until 1975.[91] During the war, the IIAF leadership apparently had the advantage of at least decent tactical photoreconnaissance from Iran's one RF-4E squadron. Early in the war, an F-4 was downed while attacking Iraqi units along the road from the border to Khorramshahr. An Iraqi commander noted, "We found detailed maps of the area in the airplane with our positions clearly earmarked on it."[92]

An assessment of both air forces' support to ground forces must conclude that neither were vital to success or defeat nor were they particularly effective. Neither air force used fixed-wing assets in a true CAS role, preferring instead to leave that role to attack helicopters that were used regularly but not in large numbers. In the interdiction role, both sides caused considerable damage but did not appear to have much effect on the course of the ground battles. The IIAF probably achieved the greater level of damage due to better tactical reconnaissance, better munitions, and more overall effort put into the interdiction role. But in the ground support role, as in all other offensive roles, both the IQAF and IIAF soon backed away from a continued effort as losses began to mount and airpower to both sides seemed less and less the key to victory. Nevertheless, both still reasoned that it could be used to avoid defeat.

## Command and Control—Different Approaches

"Centralized control, decentralized execution." This is the American airman's creed on how best to use airpower. It is enshrined in AFM 1–1, which states:

> The principles of centralized control; decentralized execution; and coordinated effort, common doctrine, and cooperation are unique to aerospace power. They are fundamental to the success of our operations.[93]

The basic tenets of this creed are simple enough. The flexibility and potential decisiveness of airpower require it be controlled by a single commander who is located at a level high enough to give the air commander an overview of the entire military situation. Ideally, once the air commander decides on how airpower will be employed, he assigns tasks to be accomplished by subordinate elements consistent with their capabilities to accomplish these tasks. The subordinate elements then decide on how best to accomplish these tasks, thus freeing the overall commander from detailed planning requirements and allowing him to concentrate on overall objectives. Coordinated effort, common doctrine, and cooperation are all givens in this equation. To more than a generation of American airmen, this is the only sensible way to employ airpower; any other approaches seem either illogical or incomprehensible. The fact that Iran and Iraq do, in fact, employ their airpower in their own style makes their actions puzzling to many informed US observers.

During the days of the shah, the IIAF worked under a centralized control and centralized execution concept. The shah was the center of all control mechanisms. He was more than a titular commander in chief since he was usually in direct personal control of operations.[94] Consequently, IIAF officers at their units were rarely given the opportunity to execute orders on their own; they were told how they would do things. Long exposure to this system reduced initiative through the command officer corps and resulted, in the late 1970s, in an IIAF command structure that inhibited independent action without detailed guidance from above.

After the revolution, command arrangements in the IIAF changed dramatically. Officers, because of their close identification with the shah, were not trusted by the new regime. Until the outbreak of war, they were used as advisers—not commanders. Effective, if nebulous, control over IIAF activities now was in the hands of either local mullahs or revolutionary committees.

The dramatic changes that had occurred to the IIAF between 1978 and 1980 and the experiences of the war gave the IIAF the opportunity to break out of the overcentralized mode of operation, but it is questionable whether it has done so. More likely, the IIAF has reverted to its previous style of excessive centralization as the mullahs in Tehran have assumed the shah's concern with security and do not want to allow any growth of independent power centers which may oppose their control. One indication that the new Iranian political leadership was determined to keep the regular military under its thumb was a 16 October 1980 announcement that required all statements about the war, including those released on military affairs by the joint staff, from that date forward go first through the propaganda committee of the mullah-dominated Supreme Defense Council.[95] But an even more telling indicator was the purging of the IIAF that took place in the late summer of 1981 after Iran's elected president, Abol Hasan Bani-Sadr, felt compelled by events to flee the country. That he did so in an IIAF transport caused the regime remaining in Tehran to remove politically suspect elements from their air force while the country was in the midst of a war. Unsure of IIAF loyalties, the regime felt it necessary to keep the IIAF under very close control.[96]

Rigid centralization appeared to be the norm on the Iraqi side as well, both before and during the war. As previously mentioned, political considerations and the need to keep military capabilities under tight political control dictated that the Baath Party keep the Iraqi military on a very short rein. No innovative behavior on the part of the IQAF was discernable. On the contrary, IQAF operations, like those of the entire Iraqi military, appeared to do only that which the political leadership specifically directed. The IQAF obviously did not take the fight to the IIAF; Iraqi fighters in combat air patrols over Iraq seemed content to bore holes in the sky rather than to seek out readily available IIAF targets.[97] Since late 1980 (when the Iraqi military effectively ceased offensive operations) through mid-1982, the IQAF (or the political leadership that controls it) has seemed content generally to not engage in combat as long as the IIAF does the same.

# NOTES

1. Air Force Manual (AFM) 1–1, *Functions and Basic Doctrine of the United States Air Force*, 14 February 1979.
2. Ibid., 2–7.
3. "Why Aren't the Iraqis Going for the Artery?" *The Economist* 277, no. 7154 (11 October 1980): 44.
4. T. R. Milton, "Where the Cauldron Boiled Over," *Air Force Magazine* 64, no. 1 (January 1981): 99.
5. AFM 1–1, 14 February 1979, 3–2.
6. Ibid., 3–3 and 3–4.
7. *IISS 80-81*, 42–43.
8. "Iranian/Iraqi Air Strikes Appear at 'Limited' Level," *AWST* 113 (6 October 1980): 20.
9. Robert Bailey, "Iraq Covets Opponents' Weaponry," *MEED* 24, no. 43 (24 October 1980): 7.
10. Tomasek, 209.
11. *FBIS-SAS-80*, 25 August 1980, Tehran newspaper *Keyhan* in Persian.
12. John Kifner, "Iranian Jets Said to Damage Several Oil Plants," *NYT*, 3 October 1980, A10; "Shipments of Oil to Mediterranean Stopped by Iraqis," *WSJ*, 29 September 1980, 2; "Damage to Iran, Iraq Oil Facilities Feared Extensive," *WSJ*, 8 October 1980, 2.
13. Robert D. Hershey, Jr., "Iraq Halts Export of Its Oil as Result of Damage by Iran," *NYT*, 27 September 1980, 1.
14. David Bird, "3 Americans Feared Dead in Air Raid on Iraqi Plant," *NYT*, 25 September 1980, A13.
15. Kifner, "Baghdad Says Its Troops Capture Khorramshahr and Cut a Rail Line," *NYT*, 26 September 1980, 1.
16. "Fakuri on Air Force Operations," *FBIS-SAS-80*, Tehran radio broadcast in Persian at 2104 GMT, 23 September 1980.
17. "Defense Minister Reports an Iraqi-Iranian Dispute," *FBIS-MEA-80-189*, INA in Arabic at 1310 GMT, 25 September 1980.
18. AFGC 61, *FBIS-MEA-80-196*, INA in Arabic at 1545 GMT, 6 October 1980.
19. "AFP: Bombing of Iraqi Oil Facilities to Continue," *FBIS-SAS-80-243*, Agence France Presse (AFP) in English at 1744 GMT, 15 December 1980.

20. "Text of Radio Interview with Commander Afzali," *FBIS-SAS-80-233*, Tehran radio broadcast in Arabic at 1800 GMT, 1 December 1980.

21. "Press Report Details Iranian Losses in Equipment," *FBIS-MEA-80-223*, INA in Arabic at 1635 GMT, 15 November 1980; AFGC 9, *FBIS-MEA-80-187*, Baghdad radio broadcast in Arabic at 1723 GMT, 23 September 1980; AFGC 11, *FBIS-MEA-80-187*, Baghdad radio broadcast in Arabic at 0540 GMT, 24 September 1980.

22. "High Official Insists War Aims Limited," *FBIS-MEA-80-201*, Kuwait *As-Siyasah* in Arabic, 9 October 1980, 15.

23. "Saddam Husayn Address to National Assembly 4 November," *FBIS-MEA-80-216*, Baghdad radio broadcast in Arabic at 1704 GMT, 4 November 1980.

24. "As War Comes to Teheran, People Scurry to Stock Up," *NYT*, 25 September 1980, A16.

25. "In Teheran, Enforced Blackouts; In Baghdad, Lively Nonchalance: The War is Hailed in Iraq," *NYT*, 30 September 1980, 1; Terry Povey, "Fighting to a Stalemate," *The Middle East* 74 (December 1980): 27.

26. Henry Tanner, "Khomeini Dismisses Truce Offer, Vowing a Fight 'To the End'," *NYT*, 1 October 1980, 1; Kifner, "Iranian Jets," *NYT*, 3 October 1980.

27. "Shipments," *WSJ*, 29 September 1980.

28. Marvine Howe, "Iraqis Resume Pumping of Oil by Pipeline Across Turkey," *NYT*, 21 November 1980, A14.

29. "Iranians Bomb Dam in Iraq's Kurd Area," *NYT*, 22 November 1980, 4.

30. "Navy Commander on Gulf Islands, War with Iraq," *FBIS-SAS-80-242*, Tehran radio broadcast in Arabic at 1855 GMT, 13 December 1980.

31. Drew Middleton, "Factor in Iraqi Push: Iranian Exiles' Aid," *NYT*, 27 September 1980, 4.

32. "Iranian/Iraqi Air Strikes," *AWST*, 6 October 1980.

33. Dupuy, 245–46.

34. "Unexploded Ordnance Warning," *FBIS-SAS-80*, Tehran radio broadcast in Persian at 1735 GMT, 22 September 1980; "Civil Defense Instructions to Citizens," *FBIS-MEA-80-187*, Baghdad radio broadcast in Arabic at 0807 GMT, 23 September 1980; "Tariq Aziz Speaks on Economy, Reagan, USSR Stand," *FBIS-MEA-80-224*, Paris *al-Mustaqbal* in Arabic, 15 November 1980.

35. O'Ballance, "The Iraqi-Iranian War: The First Round," *Parameters* 11, no. 1 (March 1981): 58.

36. "MiG-23 Draws Iraqi Complaints," *Strategy Week* 6, no. 41 (13-19 October 1980): 4.

37. See chapter 1, section on *Lesson—1956*.

38. Richard Halloran, "Iraq Said to Send Planes to Foreign Havens," *NYT*, 3 October 1980, A10; "Spokesman Denies Israeli Radio Allegation on Iraqi Planes," *FBIS-MEA-80-188*, Amman, Jordan radio broadcast in Arabic at 1600 GMT, 23 September 1980; Walter S. Mossberg, "N. Korea, Syria Are Helping Iran, US Sources Say," *WSJ*, 9 October 1980, 4.

39. Robert Graham, *Iran: The Illusion of Power* (New York: St. Martin's Press, 1979), 179 and ff.

40. Saddam Hussein, *Social and Foreign Affairs in Iraq*, trans. by Khalid Kishtainy (London: Croom Helm, Ltd., 1979), 92.

41. Tanner, "Jordan Acts to Aid Iraq with Supplies for War with Iran," *NYT*, 7 October 1980, 1.

42. "Iranian Armed Forces Joint General Staff Announcement No. 82," *FBIS-SAS-80*, Tehran radio broadcast in Persian at 1030 GMT, 28 September 1980 (hereafter referred to as JGS, followed by the number).

43. Insight Team of the London *Sunday Times*, *The Yom Kippur War* (Garden City, N.Y.: Doubleday & Co., Inc., 1974), 200–4.

44. Eric Rouleau, "Interview with Bani-Sadr (no date)," *FBIS-SAS-80-197*, Paris *LeMonde* in French, 8 October 1980; Drew Middleton, "Air War's Emerging Role," *NYT*, 9 October 1980, A16.

45. Drew Middleton, "Factor in Iraqi Push," *NYT*.

46. "Iraqi Tank Guns Stop Missile Helicopters," *AWST* 113 (24 November 1980): 66.

47. "AFP: Iranian AF Bombs Baghdad," *FBIS-MEA-80-191*, Paris AFP in English at 1038 GMT, 30 September 1980; "Iranian Planes Bomb Baghdad Outskirts 14 October," *FBIS-MEA-80-201*, Paris AFP in

English at 1230 GMT, 14 October 1980; "Iranian Bombing of Baghdad Resumes 17 October," *FBIS-MEA-80-203*, Paris AFP in English at 1008 GMT, 17 October 1980.

48. "Phantom Attack on Baghdad," *FBIS-MEA-80-188*, Hong Kong AFP in English at 0935 GMT, 25 September 1980; "BBC Reports on Iranian Air Attacks Against Baghdad 25 September," *FBIS-MEA-80-189*, BBC World Service in English at 1500 GMT, 25 September 1980; "AFP: Iranian AF Bombs Baghdad," *FBIS-MEA-80-191*, Paris AFP in English at 0642 GMT, 27 September 1980; "Iranian Bombing of Baghdad Resumes," *FBIS-MEA-80-203*; David Fairhall, "The Iran-Iraq War at First Hand," *Defense Week* 1, no. 31 (3 November 1980): 5; David R. Griffiths, "Iran Begins to Use Cobras, Mavericks," *AWST* 113 (13 October 1980): 24.

49. "BBC Reports on Iranian Air Attacks," *FBIS-MEA-80-189*; Kifner, "Amid Confusion of Battle, Iraqis Press On," *NYT*, 28 September 1980, 1; Kifner, "Iraqi Oil Center Damaged," *NYT*, 30 September 1980, A14.

50. Fairhall, 5.

51. "Iraqi Tank Guns," *AWST* 113 (24 November 1980): 66; Halloran, "Iranians' Effectiveness in Fighting Iraq is Astonishing U.S. Military Analysts," *NYT*, 15 October 1980, A14.

52. Drew Middleton, "Tactics in Gulf War," *NYT*, 19 October 1980, 12.

53. "Iran Using F-14 in 'Mini-AWACS' Role," *Aerospace Daily* 105, no. 30 (14 October 1980): 236; "Iraq Using US AWACS Link: Iran Uses F-14," *Strategy Week* 6, no. 42 (20–26 October 1980): 5.

54. "Iraqi SAMs," *Strategy Week* 7, no. 2 (19-25 January 1981): 1; "Iraq Asks France for Crotale," *International Defense Intelligence Newsletter (DMS)*, 3 November 1980, 2; "Iraqis Negotiating Rapier Buy?" *International Defense Intelligence Newsletter (DMS)*, 22 December 1980, 3; "Iraqi Want Roland," *International Defense Intelligence Newsletter (DMS)*, 30 March 1981, 3; "Air Force to Have Franco-German SAM Missiles," *FBIS-MEA-81-043*, Paris *LeMonde* in French, 3 March 1981.

55. "French Missiles Adapted to Soviet Aircraft," *FBIS-MEA-81-065*, Paris *LeMonde* in French, 28 April 1981; "MiG-25s Equipped with Magic Missiles?" *International Defense Newsletter (DMS)*, 8 June 1981, 3.

56. Frank J. Prime, "France Confirms Reports It Has Handed Over 4 Mirage Jets to Iraqis," *NYT*, 2 February 1981, A6.

57. AFM 1–1, 14 February 1979, para. 1-7.

58. Ibid., para. 6–4.

59. Examples of this belief can be found in Gen William W. Momyer, *Airpower in Three Wars* (Washington, D.C.: Government Printing Office, January 1978); and in the series of articles by Drew Middleton in the *New York Times* during late 1980 and 1981.

60. See chapter on IQAF history.

61. Senate, *US Military Sales to Iran*, 25.

62. Personal interview with former chief of Air Section/ ARMISH-MAAG Iran.

63. Momyer, 111.

64. AFM 1–1, 14 February 1979, 2–15.

65. See Shazly, 19, 273.

66. "President Id al-Adha Message to People, Armed Forces," *FBIS-MEA-80-204*, Baghdad radio broadcast in Arabic at 2115 GMT, 8 October 1980.

67. AFM 2–1, 2 May 1969, para. 5-2.

68. Ibid., para. 5-4.

69. "Non-Iranian Aircraft Thought to Have Attacked Iraq," *FBIS-MEA-80-192*, London Ash-Sharq al-Awsat in Arabic, 30 September 1980.

70. AFM 2–1, 2 May 1969, para. 4-2.

71. Kifner, "Iraqi Planes Strike 10 Airfields in Iran: Oil Area Imperiled," *NYT*, 23 September 1980, 1.

72. Shazly, 115, 127.

73. Ibid., 158, 274.

74. Iraqi and Iranian claims in *FBIS*.

75. "Khamene'i Comments (via announcer)," *FBIS-SAS-80*, Tehran radio broadcast in Arabic at 0800 GMT, 23 September 1980.

76. Kifner, "Iraqi Planes Strike 10 Airfields in Iran: Oil Area Imperiled," *NYT*, 23 September 1980, A12.

77. "Bani-Sadr Speech," *FBIS-SAS-80*, Tehran radio broadcast in Persian at 1525 GMT, 22 September 1980.

78. JGS 54, *FBIS-SAS-80*, Tehran radio broadcast in Persian at 1030 GMT, 26 September 1980.

79. JGS 82, *FBIS-SAS-80*.

80. For example, see Kifner, "Attacking Iraqi Troops in Iran Find the Foe Still Fights," *NYT*, 1 October 1980, A10; Drew Middleton, "Iraq's Waning Attack," *NYT*, 2 October 1980, A16; Kifner, "Iranian Jets Said to Damage Several Iraqi Oil Plants," *NYT*, 3 October 1980, A10.

81. *IISS 80-81*, 42.

82. As indicated in their daily claims as reported by *FBIS*.

83. Rouleau, "Khorramshahr and Abadan Virtually Cut-off from Rest of Country," *FBIS-SAS-80-203*, Paris *LeMonde* in French, 16 October 1980.

84. "Iraqi Tank Guns Stop Missile Helicopters," *AWST* 113 (24 November 1980): 66.

85. According to Iraqi claims as reported by *FBIS*.

86. JGS 480, *FBIS-SAS-81-080*, Tehran radio broadcast in Persian at 2030 GMT, 24 April 1981.

87. Described in their daily battle statements as reported by *FBIS*.

88. Kifner, "Attacking Iraqi Troops."

89. David Ignatius, "Vignettes of War: Phantom and Taxi; Suspicion in Basra," *WSJ*, 3 October 1980, 1.

90. Jacques Meral, "AFP Correspondent Describes Khuzestan Fighting," *FBIS-SAS-80-195*, Paris AFP in English at 1925 GMT, 4 October 1980.

91. Personal interview with former chief of Air Section/ ARMISH-MAAG.

92. Youssef M. Ibrahim, "Iraq and Iran Battle for Key Cities; A War of Attrition Appears Likely," *NYT*, 4 October 1980, 1.

93. AFM 1-1, 14 February 1976, para. 5-3, 94; Graham, 170.

95. "Statement on News Coordination," *FBIS-SAS-80-203*, Tehran radio broadcast in Persian at 1030 GMT, 16 October 1980.

96. "Acting Air Force Chief on Changes in AF," *FBIS-SAS-81-156*, Tehran radio broadcast in Persian at 1030 GMT, 12 August 1981.

97. "Intelligence Limited," *AWST* 113 (13 October 1980): 24.

# CHAPTER 6

# Conclusions

"The war, they believe, will be war in the air."[1] That was the conventional wisdom in the fall of 1980. By 1982, the Iran-Iraq war had receded from the front pages and from the minds of many US airmen who, if they cared any longer, usually felt that the war could have been won in the air had the antagonists only used the correct strategies and tactics. But did US Air Force observers recognize the role of airpower in this war?

In previous chapters of this study, we looked at the historical backgrounds of the two air forces which participated in this war. We noted Iraqi participation in the Arab wars with Israel, and we postulated that IQAF behavior in the war with Iran was conditioned in part by the airpower lessons the Arab states had taken from their experiences against the IAF. We also noted that a historical involvement in domestic politics had undermined IQAF professionalism. On the other side, we noted that the IIAF was, in reality, a quite new, untested organization in 1980. It was forced into combat with most of its top command layer having been thrust only recently into positions of major responsibility. We looked at IQAF and IIAF combat behavior and deduced that while both air forces are subordinate to their respective armies in their organizational hierarchies, their most important mission, in reality, is *not* the direct support of ground forces. Rather, the most important mission for both air forces is to deter the enemy from escalating the conflict in strategic terms. Both air forces, therefore, were used primarily to keep the war limited in scope and intensity. When deterrence is the primary air force role, the maintenance of that deterrent capability (and hence, credibility) becomes all important. Thus attrition becomes a vital consideration; the losses incurred as a by-product of offensive initiative cause the air forces to willingly give up offensive initiative and replace it with a conservative—even stylized and ritualistic—defensive posture.

This chapter concludes the study on the use of airpower in the Iran-Iraq war by discussing three topic areas. First, it discusses the role that airpower played as a part of the military instrument wielded by the political leaderships in Baghdad and Tehran; it notes the power that political considerations had over military needs. Second, accepting these political strictures, this study deduces the Iraqi and Iranian approaches to airpower within the general context of these strictures. This is done by looking at how IQAF and IIAF behavior contrasts with US Air Force principles of war. Comments are also presented on the impact that cultural influences have on military considerations. Finally, an attempt is made to state what the foregoing means for the US Air Force.

## The Role of Airpower

Did American observers recognize the role of airpower in this war? Further, did American observers recognize the role the military instrument played in the strategic decisions made in Baghdad and Tehran? Informed writers like T.R. Milton, the analysts who gave their opinions to journalists like Drew Middleton, and many, if not most, American airmen (this author was definitely included in the majority) have looked at this particular war pretty much as a military affair. Such groups wanted to view the Iran-Iraq war as the military execution of national objectives as established by the respective political leaderships. In such a situation, prosecution of the war fell to the military forces who sought to accomplish those objectives through the application of military power. Moreover, we wanted to understand Iranian and Iraqi air operations as driven by military necessities, unfettered by constant civilian political tinkering. But as we saw in chapter 3, the Iraqi military, at least, was used within very tight political constraints; and when initial estimates proved erroneous, the Iraqi military was told, in essence, "Don't try to win the war; just hang on, and don't lose it while we try to figure a way out of this mess." This situation makes any real understanding of the Iraqi (and to some extent the Iranian since Iran reacted to Iraqi moves) way of air war problematic. Given a different scenario, both sides may well act in a different manner. It must be truthfully said, however, that a different manner may yield no better results than did their style in this war.

## Strategic Considerations

The employment of airpower is only one aspect of the use of military force, and military force is only one aspect of the total strategic equation. Total strategy entails far more than pure military strategy. For instance, one of the most important strategic considerations—for Iraq more so than for Iran—was the need to keep the conflict limited in violence, area, and participants. If Iran collapsed after Iraq's first application of military power, then total victory was attainable. But if Iran did not collapse after Iraq's initial application of military power, then an attempt to gain total victory would jeopardize Iraq's strategic objectives. One thing Iraq did not want to happen was to have the superpowers enter the arena because their interests appeared threatened. If Iraq had the capability to grind down Iran and Iran began over time to crumble, began to lose its territorial integrity, then the Soviet Union would invoke its 1921 treaty with Iran as a pretext to step in and to take effective control of this major Middle Eastern state.[2] Such a move would not be in the long-term interests of Baghdad.

Therefore, Iraq military action had to be limited if it became apparent that the Islamic regime was not a house of cards, ripe for destruction. The war had to be won quickly if external actors were to be kept out. It was not, and Iraq essentially lost the war somewhere around 5 October 1980 at which time it began looking for a way out.

Compounding Iraq's strategic problem was the fact that Tehran could precipitate outside intervention. Tehran, if faced with the destruction of its precious Islamic revolution and the potential loss of its oil, could conceivably follow through on its stated threats[3] and lash out, striking at Arab oil producers in the Gulf in an effort to hurt them as Iran was being hurt. Such an action would invite both US and Soviet attention, ranging from an imposed settlement and to an actual takeover of "the world's oil" from its obviously capable and untrustworthy stewards. Paranoid feelings along these lines were easily fed by articles which had appeared in the West since 1973 suggesting the necessity for the West to straighten out the oil mess. And would the Soviets want to watch that happen without dividing the spoils? In such a situation, the combatants put unstated, but consensual, limits on their military actions. Military operations became as important for what they are—signals—as for what they may accomplish. Western observers could see it happening, but did not want to admit it. T. R. Milton stated the common feeling in a January 1981 article in *Air Force Magazine* when he said, "Unlikely though it may be, the thought occurs that the Iraqis are trying the sort of air warfare—whatever did we call it: giving signals?—that our politicians devised in the 1960s."[4]

When Iran eased off on the strategic punishment strikes, Iraq did the same. Strategic attacks from November 1980 on took on a ritualistic quality; Iran "destroyed" Iraq's offshore loading platforms at Mina al-Bakr and Khor al-Amaya on a number of occasions after it first "destroyed" them at the end of November 1980. Iraq answered with ineffectual attacks on Kharg Island, sometimes hitting nothing, sometimes noncritical storage areas, but never tankers taking on oil, an act that would have shut down Iran's export operation. Similarly, Iraq's oil exports via pipeline through Turkey were generally free from disruption after reopening in late 1980. Iran's attacks on Kuwaiti custom posts on the Iraqi border were obvious signals that there were limits to how overt the other Arab states could make their aid to Iraq. The IIAF's April 1981 raid on H-3 airfield in far western Iraq also could not have gone unnoticed by other Arab governments who could find themselves within range of a refueled IIAF F-4.

For Iraq, the "efficient, rational" use of its military instrument (even if that instrument could be used efficiently, a fact that has not yet been demonstrated) had to be subservient to perceived political needs. Despite the actual or potential capabilities of the various air forces, the observations of Clausewitz bore out.

> War, therefore, is an act of policy. Were it a complete, untrameled, absolute manifestation of violence (as the pure concept would require), war would of its own independent will usurp the place of policy the moment policy had brought being; it would then drive policy out of office and rule by the laws of its own nature. . . . If we keep in mind that war springs from some political purpose, it is natural that the prime cause of its existence will remain the supreme consideration in conducting it.[5]

The Iraqis, however, seemed to disregard the remainder of Clausewitz's observation.

> That, however, does not imply that the political aim is a tyrant. It must adapt itself to its chosen means, a process which can radically change it; yet the political aim remains the first consideration. Policy, then, will permeate all military operations, and, insofar as their violent nature will admit, it will have a continuous influence on them.[6]

## Cultural Factors Impacting Strategy

The Iraqi strategic problem was compounded by several cultural factors, factors which Baghdad obviously (and perhaps fatally) undervalued. One of the most important factors was Iranian morale. While Iraq appeared to possess equal or perhaps even superior stocks of military hardware, it did not have an answer for Iranian morale and Iranian willingness to sacrifice men and materiel in order to gain victory.[7] Clausewitz, who noted the relationship between military operations and overall strategies, also noted that military hardware alone is not all that matters.

> . . . the moral elements are among the most important in war. . . . [The principal elements are] the skill of the commander, the experience and courage of the troops, and their patriotic spirit. The relative value of each cannot be universally established; it is hard enough to discuss their potential, and even more difficult to weigh them against each other. The wisest course is not to underrate any of them—a temptation to which human judgment, being fickle, often succumbs.[8]

It would appear that the Iraqis undervalued the impact of belief and will in the equation of war. They seemed to place higher values on military hardware and assume that, properly used (though their usage could hardly be considered exemplary), their equipment could destroy enough enemy equipment and allow occupation of enough land to force either a government collapse or a desire for a settlement.

A second Iranian-imposed factor, Iran's revolutionary ethic, also set back Iraqi plans. The revolution, for all its excesses, was a watershed in Iranian politics, and the revolutionary spirit infected the Iranian soldiery—especially the paramilitary Revolutionary Guards. Enough of the Iranian military and populace believed either in Khomeini, in the revolution, or in Iran to make their collective will a factor Iraq had not adequately considered. Baghdad could have found warnings about the value of will in its own Arab experience. Lt Col al-Haytham al-Ayoubi is a former Syrian officer and a military/political analyst. A comment he made explaining why the Arabs refuse to accept the fact that Israel defeats them militarily at every turn was just as applicable for Iraq in its struggle with Iran.

> In the past, occupation of territories, important cities, or vital areas signified an opponent's defeat. But in the 20th century, war is no longer a struggle between two armed forces; it is a struggle between peoples moved by strong ideological currents and rooted beliefs. These conflicts do not end when a number of villages, cities, or territories are occupied. Fighting does not stop unless the will of the opponent is shattered or bled to death, or unless intervention by other states puts an end to the fighting. This new type of war has new characteristics. Revolutionary forces may ignore the value of the land and strengthen popular resistance and morale. Given the will to fight, they may prolong the war until the enemy is tired of fighting and is convinced of the futility of settling the conflict by force of arms.[9]

A third Iranian-imposed factor was the religious issue. As noted earlier, secular Baathist Iraq was already on the defensive in an argument with an aggressive enemy fired by religious zeal. Often in Muslim history, one group of Muslims would war on another group, claiming they were apostates.[10] The same was true in this conflict, Tehran couched its rhetoric in terms of believers (Iranians) fighting unbelievers (Baathist Iraqis). Such a situation complicated Iraqi hopes for a termination of hostilities. In a fight where one side thinks they are fighting for Islam, cessation of hostilities can only come with a victory for the Islamic side. Shia Islam, especially, holds negotiations with "infidels" in particularly poor esteem. In such a situation, Iraqi offers of cease-fires and negotiations were bound to be ignored by Tehran; victory was the only acceptable outcome for the Iranian religious leadership. Muslim jurisprudence, however, allows hostilities to cease without an Islamic victory, but only when a superior force (or force majeure) imposes a settlement.[11] In all previous major Middle Eastern wars, force majeure in the guise of the United States and the Soviet Union was necessary to compel an end to hostilities.[12] Baghdad did not want superpower intrusion into the region, and the superpowers were content to let Iran and Iraq batter each other senseless as long as their spat did not threaten Western or Soviet interests. Thus Iraq was stuck with a war it could not or would not win against an enemy that could accept only victory or force majeure imposition of a settlement—both anathema to Baghdad.

## Airpower Approaches

Both countries (and their air forces), however, displayed some general tendencies, tendencies that they may again exhibit in foreseeable future conflicts. In a purely military sense, devoid of the political constraints or limitations of this war, what do the Iraqis and Iranians view as the value of airpower, the utility of airpower? Do they see it as the US Air Force does, as a primary key to military victory or success? The Iraqis apparently do not—at least not in the offensive mode the US Air Force views as essential to success. The Iraqi approach to military success appears to be a continental approach similar to the approach used by other Arab states, most notably Egypt. For them, the essence of victory is occupation, physical possession of real estate. Because the army is the only force capable of occupying territory, the army becomes the decisive military arm. The air force can help the army compel the enemy to give up real estate, but it cannot do it alone. The air force *can* be decisive but only as part of an overall military effort in which the army is the most important component.

But while this appears to be the Iraqi idea about airpower's role in achieving a decisive conclusion to conflict, the Iraqis never seemed to get to a point of decision. Rather, they seemed willing (and now in 1982 as Iranian forces have invaded Iraqi soil, seemingly remain willing) to limit airpower's role in the conflict to a point short of decisiveness. In this interim, or limited, military mode that does not foresee decisive military operations, the IQAF's most vital role is to keep the conflict limited by deterring Iran from expanding the boundaries of the conflict either in terms of geography or in terms of levels of destruction. Since the inherent capabilities of any air force allow it to do just that—expand the physical or qualitative boundaries of a conflict—then the IQAF's deterrent role is aimed primarily at the IIAF.

The Iranian approach is a bit more difficult to pin down. Iranian military thinking is undergoing a period of uncertainty, and doctrinal ideas about airpower are just now evolving out of prior training history, out of a still unstable revolutionary situation, and out of a measure of combat success in Iran's first major war in memory. The old line of the Iranian Air Force and military is gone. The backbone of its structure is the lieutenants, captains, and few field grade officers who, for a variety of reasons, have avoided purges and persecution and have, again for a number of causes, chosen not to leave the service and/or their country. They are flying or directing US war planes and most of them received at least their basic flying training in the United States. Some obviously have internalized US Air Force tactics (how to avoid SAMs for instance), but how much US Air Force doctrine were they exposed to and how much did they internalize? It is likely that they will depend, to a large extent, on their experiences in the war with Iraq. What do these experiences tell them? First, they may have saved Iran from defeat in the early days of the war. Second, Iran, however, was successful in expelling the Iraqi invaders without any significant air support. And third, emotional fervor and patriotism can multiply proficiency to create a military force more potent than one possessing physical capability alone.

Both countries' air forces do have some similarities, however. Both seem quite secure in using their air forces as deterrents, periodically advertising their ability to inflict a punishing blow, but preferring to keep them in reserve so the enemy will hesitate to use his air assets. Keeping the air force inbeing to preserve its deterrent role then becomes a paramount consideration. This leads to an extreme sensitivity to offensive attrition, particularly when there is little prospect of quickly replacing losses. Because offensive attrition is avoidable in many cases, it becomes the first to go when losses begin to mount. And if both sides try to avoid offensive attrition, then both can also avoid defensive attrition since they come under attack less often. And if the war remains limited enough so that neither side fears complete collapse, then imposed attrition is never imposed. The end result is that air forces remain inbeing to serve as deterrents. This need for deterrents means it is more important to keep an air force in existence for its deterrent value than it is to use that same air force in combat where losses are inevitable. Such use and, therefore, such losses not only reduce its actual capability but can also reduce its deterrent value (if losses are great) and thus might tempt an enemy to test its credibility by attacking. Hence, by using this line of reasoning, it is more important to have an air force and not use it than it is to use it and possibly lose it.

## Principles of War

One can also discuss general Iraqi and Iranian tendencies by looking at how they acted in regard to what we consider principles of war. AFM 1–1 lists eleven of them.

### 1. Objective

Did the IQAF know its military objective? Did the Iraqi political command know its military and political objectives? These questions are hard to answer. It does appear that Baghdad's overarching objective was to bring down the Khomeini regime, but whether that objective was translated into reasonable or realistic military objectives is questionable. *The Economist* offered what appeared to be a reasonable goal: "Iraq's basic military aim is, or should be if it has one, to bring the Iranian armed forces grinding to a halt by cutting off the flow of oil."[13] But it seems more likely that Baghdad changed its objective in the midst of the war from a definition of "victory" to a "peace with honor." This political objective did not seem easily translatable into military objectives.

Tehran knew, and still knows, its objective—total victory which will occur when the Baathist regime in Baghdad is removed. Command and control problems early in the war hampered the IIAF from focusing on its military objectives and later, as it became evident that the war would not be won in the air, the IIAF's main contribution to the objective was its ability to act as a deterrent. The IIAF, however, did use its strategic airlift capability to transport supplies to Iran from sellers all over the world[14]—the military objective being the arming of Iran for the final victory.

## 2. Offensive

The IQAF, like other Arab air forces, does not seem to have an offensive mentality. As the war took on the aspect of trench warfare by 1981, Iraqi ground forces still faced daily shelling as Iranian ground forces massed for attacks first on the Abadan-Bandar-e Khomeini road, then around Abadan, and finally across the Karun River against Khorramshahr. There is no doubt the Iraqi ground forces would have appreciated some effective interdiction support, but IQAF activity appeared spotty and none too preemptive. (In fact, reported IQAF activity in the summer 1982 Iranian invasion seemed concentrated on attacks outside the battle zone. The IQAF hit towns and economic targets in apparent strategic attacks designed to compel Iran to limit the war. The IQAF showed little offensive spirit in support of Iraqi ground forces.) Overall, the IQAF seemed more intent on maintaining a defensive mentality. This predilection for the defensive is, in part, conditioned by IQAF equipment—short-range, light payload attack aircraft and a preponderance of interceptors in their fighter force.

The IIAF, as long as it can maintain a minimum number of aircraft and crews, will remain a more capable offensive force whose long-range, heavy payload F-4s have both an aerial refueling capability and sophisticated offensive armament like Maverick air-to-ground missiles. The IIAF carried the war to Iraq in the early days, but attrition caused it to back off. The IIAF seemed to have the will for the offensive but was forced away from it by attrition; in contrast, the IQAF did not seem to have the will and backed off because the IIAF did.

## 3. Mass

This was the one principle of war that both sides absolutely, consistently disregarded. Neither air force ever massed its forces; rather both sides constantly piecemealed them. At no time were there more than six or so aircraft in a single attack; very few times did there occur a rapid follow-on attack. Moreover, nowhere did either side mass its forces to overwhelm target defenses. A lot of aircraft were seen but never a lot of aircraft at one time. Such repetitious, small attacks achieved very little other than reparable damage. Iran claimed in December 1980 that Kharg Island had been hit by repeated raids, but little damage had occurred.[15] Each attack involved only a few planes, carrying only a few bombs, and they always faced target defenses. Iran's constant one- and two-plane F-5 raids into northern Iraq achieved the same sort of results—a little damage but nothing catastrophic. Neither air force ever massed its forces into a fist that could deliver a knockout punch or even a telling body blow. Both seemed content to use a few planes at a time in a kind of mutual face-slapping exercise—foolish and irritating but hardly decisive.

## 4. Economy of Force

If one viewed this as the converse of mass, then both the IQAF and IIAF seemed well versed in this principle. While both seemed to overemphasize economy of force, it is quite possible the IIAF was forced to economize carefully because it did not have too much force to work with (especially qualified pilots). On balance, however, both air forces seemed well versed on the "no-more-than-necessary" aspect of economy of force but did not show too much grasp of the corollary, "no less."

## 5. Surprise

The IQAF certainly started with surprise on 22 September 1980, but its failure to use mass to maintain the offensive negated the effectiveness of its surprise. Both air forces used surprise when they flew so low that air defense systems seemed unable to track them. The IQAF penetrated successfully all the way to Tehran each time it tried. The IIAF was equally successful in penetrating to Baghdad. Iran's raid on H-3 airfields in western Iraq was certainly a surprise to the IQAF. But again, the failure to mass enough aircraft for the attack reduced it to an example of good IIAF planning that resulted in a tap-on-the-shoulder gesture in terms of concrete results.

## 6. Security

It is hard to comment on this principle other than to say that the consistent ability of both air forces to get to their targets with minimal interference would indicate the enemy was not able to seize on a security lapse to lay in wait.

## 7. Unity of Effort

For the US Air Force, unity of effort means central control of air assets in order to best employ them to gain overall success. Both Iran and Iraq showed very little unity of effort; they generally dissipated the potential effectiveness of the air-ground team by having the air forces when they were needed. For example, the IQAF was noticeably absent when Iraqi ground forces were invading Iran. A major reason for this lack of aerial support may be structural; both air forces seem to believe that air defense assets in army hands are equally lethal to foe and friend alike.

## 8. Maneuver

Again, the US Air Force considers maneuver as a way to maintain the initiative. Maintenance of the initiative does not, however, seem to be a high priority for the IQAF or IIAF. It is entirely probable that individual pilots used maneuver as a way of maintaining initiative in air-to-air combat, but the fact that IQAF and IIAF CAPs seemed willing to orbit practically in sight of each other without initiating combat tends to indicate that both air forces accord a low priority on a larger scale maneuver (and initiative).[16]

### 9. Simplicity

Both the IQAF and IIAF seem to hold this principle dear. Except for the H-3 raid (which appeared to entail at least two aerial refuelings and apparently took liberties with Turkish and Syrian airspace sovereignty), almost all IIAF and IQAF offensive operations seemed straightforwardly simple—close-in, single-pass, hit-and-run missions by few aircraft, apparently similar in type and using similar munitions. Both sides seemed to recognize their structural limitations and took pains not to compound their problems by complicating their operations.

### 10. Timing and Tempo

Unlike the US Air Force, which uses timing and tempo to double its efforts in order to overwhelm a slower adversary, both the Iraqis and Iranians appeared incapable of (or indifferent to) keeping up a quick pace across the spectrum of missions. In fact, their attack missions took on a cyclical look as each reacted to the other rather than forcing the issue.

### 11. Defensive

Like economy of force and simplicity, they tended to overdo this principle since they seemed to prefer to sit back and fend off blows; they did not seem to accept the fact that "defense alone won't win." But perhaps that view brings us full cycle; they do not seem to expect their air forces to win the war, they only expect them to help avoid losing it.

## Cultural Factors Impacting Military Operations

In this conflict, the Iraqi military effort especially seemed hampered by several factors. One of the most important factors that limited Baghdad's ability to pursue this war to a successful conclusion was that Iraqi military professionalism suffered from too much politicization of the officer corps. As noted in chapter 2, this has been a disabling fact of life for the IQAF, but it has also hurt most all Arab military organizations in the period since World War II. Pakistani author S. A. el-Edroos succinctly captured the essence of the Iraqi (and Arab) problem.

> [There are] cogent reasons for the apparent lack of leadership and professionalism in the Arab officer cadre. The political upheavals which plagued the Arab world in the tumultuous post-war years siphoned off large segments of the professional officer cadre to the disabling field of politics . . . the professional quality of the Arab armies suffered

severely from the constant drain and elimination of the officer cadre, drawn into the vortex of domestic politics and the struggle for power. In many cases, relatively junior officers were catapulted into positions of responsibility for which they were totally lacking in experience and knowledge.[17]

The Arab, and hence the Iraqi, problem with professionalism is seen in its most striking contrast when compared with the Israeli experience.

From 1953 on, command of the IAF remained in the capable hands of a highly motivated, imaginative, and dedicated professional cadre of air force commanders. These men concentrated their efforts on fashioning the IAF into the effective and efficient instrument of war it proved to be.[18]

The Israelis have come to grips with the realities and conditions of modern Middle Eastern warfare, but it seems that some Arab militaries (the Iraqi, for example) have remained mired in outdated patterns of behavior. The author does not want to put undue stress on this aspect, but it appears that some of the ageless Bedouin style of warfare has continued to the present day in the subconscious mind of Arab soldiers where it affects their military performance. The military style (if not the equipment) of the Bedouin of the Arabian desert has remained fairly unchanged for thousands of years—one anthropologist refers to it as "a mechanism of ecological adaptation."[19] The style of the desert Bedouin raiders is based on a surprise attack followed by a quick retreat to evade pursuit or capture. The early Muslim warriors used this style in their conquest of the area now known as Iraq. Raiders out of the desert fell upon settled communities, plundered them, then retreated into the desert with their booty. Where settlements were defended, the raiders menaced the livelihood of the settlement by carrying off livestock and threatening destruction of crops. In very few cases did the attackers ever choose to assault a settlement or a strong point; in most cases, the settlements capitulated to the attackers' demands which were usually not too exorbitant.[20] Raids such as these remained a fact of life for Iraq up to the 1930s.[21]

Parallels to this style of warfare can be noted in the Iran-Iraq war of 1980–81, some thirteen and a half centuries after the original Muslim conquest of Iraq. IQAF air raids had in them the surprise attack, the quick retreat quality of the Bedouin raids. Iraqi threats to destroy Iranian oil and populated areas in Khuzistan remind one of Bedouin threats to destroy crops, and the Iraqi preference for static artillery exchanges over closing with the enemy in the cities of Khuzistan reminds one of the Bedouin preference for threats instead of pitched battle as a means of forcing capitulation.

But the early Muslims had two distinct elements in their armies. One was the Bedouin raiders, the cavalry—mobile and swift but unreliable in a contested battle. The other was the townsmen. Lacking the ability or skills to be mobile raiders, they were more suited for stubborn defense. The Prophet Mohammad used these attributes in his victory at the Battle of Badr in 624 A.D. His forces (mostly townsmen) took control of the only wells in the area, then invited a thirsty and desperate enemy to attack them.[22] This preference for using the stolid townsmen in a defensive mode was echoed thirteen and a half centuries later on the Suez front in 1973 where the Egyptian army intended to take a portion of the Sinai, then settle back in defense to allow the Israeli army to destroy itself by attacking the Egyptian defenses. The same behavior could be seen among the Iraqis in 1980–81. The army seemed willing to dig in and invite Iranian attack, while the IQAF seemed to prefer ground-based air defense over offensive counterair as a way to destroy the IIAF.

It is transparently obvious that military equipment, training, and organization have changed dramatically over the ages since the dawn of Islam, but it appears to this author that some of the old Arab ways of warfare have continued over time in the subconscious of Arab leaders. Comparing Iraqi actions in 1980–81 with Arab actions in the seventh century A.D., one can note parallels that explain (at least in part) some Iraqi actions in the war with Iran.

\* \* \* \* \* \* \* \* \* \*

The war, this author believed, would be won in the air. Like other American airmen, conditioned by experiences within the US Air Force structure, I felt the Iraqis could use their airpower to knock Iran right out of the war. Airpower, used in a sensible fashion, could eliminate all that tiresome slogging through the mud of Khuzistan. A strong counterair effort could gain air superiority and dedicated interdiction of pipelines and pumping stations leading to Kharg Island could bankrupt Tehran. Iraq, with rich friends and large bank accounts, could easily wait out Iranian efforts to hurt its oil industry. I did not want to see anything other than a military operation.

But now, recognizing the war was not won in the air and recognizing there were limits and constraints that conditioned the employment of airpower in this conflict, are there any lessons we can draw from this war? I feel there are some lessons that can be learned, but they are not like those of the 1973 war; they are not the dramatic tactical developments that are testable against our own doctrine and tactics. The results of the Iran-Iraq air war do not seriously challenge our own beliefs about the efficacy of airpower. Neither air force held to the offensive, but the offensive still seems the key to victory in this war as well as in any foreseeable conflict. True, each side tried to use its air force to avoid defeat, but that is a static effort. In the end, it was Iranian infantry offensive operations that drove Iraqi invaders out. The Iraqi ground forces could well have stayed or advanced had the IQAF eliminated the IIAF threat by use of fighter sweeps, for example, and followed up with interdiction efforts against Iranian rear areas which would have then been devoid of effective air cover. But the IQAF did not, and thus the Iraqi army had to withdraw.

\* \* \* \* \* \* \* \* \* \*

The IIAF and IQAF tendencies toward defensive/deterrent operations indicate that should US Air Force elements ever have to operate in this area with them as enemies, the US Air Force would not see too much Iraqi or Iranian efforts aimed at taking out US air assets. While robust point defense around US Air Force installations would be beneficial, an early and strong US Air Force counterair effort could effectively eliminate any IQAF or IIAF desire to initiate a counterair campaign of their own. Neither the IQAF nor the IIAF seems convinced it can carry out the offensive counterair role; hence, US efforts might well be carried out with minimal enemy pressure except when the US Air Force chooses to force the action. The US Air Force could determine the time and place of battle and could maintain the initiative because neither the IQAF nor the IIAF seems interested in it themselves.

How could this affect US Air Force operations? First, if the US Air Force could achieve a 1967-type elimination of their air assets, then by all means this should be a top priority. But if a 1967 appears just out of our reach, then the US Air Force might want to hit them hard enough so that they hold back to preserve their airframes, but not so hard that we drive them to desperation. The US Air Force could effectively remove them from the battle without forcing them into an imposed attrition situation. Short of imposed attrition, they would be willing to avoid confrontation if they could remain somewhat intact. Forcing them to the wall would make them more stalwart in their resistance (even if they proved to be foolishly brave as was the Egyptian Air Force in 1973 when the Israeli threat to the Third Army forced it to fly missions it would have preferred to avoid).

With the IQAF or IIAF as allies during military operations in this arena, their tendencies would make them useful to an air campaign but only in limited aspects. More so than the Iranians, the Iraqis (and by extension other Arabs) would look with disfavor on US Air Force attempts to push them into an offensive role. They would be much more inclined to accept the defensive—or covering—role, thereby freeing more US Air Force assets for the offensive role. Even though their ability in either the offensive or defensive role may be limited and even though their aircraft may be well suited for an offensive role, they would prefer the defensive role and mission.

But what about the US Air Force as an institution? Does this war and our understanding of it tell us anything about the US Air Force's ability to carry out national objectives when the military objective may find itself hemmed in and limited by external political considerations? Will the United States be forced in the future to act within political constraints as was the IQAF? It is hard to imagine that in this day of improved command, control, and communications ($C^3$) capabilities, the political leadership of any nation would not use that capability and try to direct military operations regardless of military objectives. One principal problem in assessing the use of airpower in the Iran-Iraq war seems to stem from the fact that often there is a tendency to view military problems as just that—pure, pristine military problems. And the necessity for military professionalism would not wish it otherwise. But perhaps in this growing environment of tighter central control over all aspects of national power—including military power—the US Air Force would do well to ponder future operations that might well be constrained by tight political control. If the Iran-Iraq air war shows us nothing else, it shows us that in limited war the flexibility of airpower allows it to be misused or overruled by political expediency; thus the challenge to airpower planners is how to devise ways to maintain the spirit of the offensive and to retain the initiative even when forced to operate in this milieu.

The author believes that wars *can* be won in the air. It will be the US Air Force's task to win that war even when, as in the Iran-Iraq war, the air effort is subordinated (perhaps even improperly subordinated) to other aspects of national strategy. However, to achieve this, US air planners must first recognize the nature of the war in which they are engaged and the realities of the political imperatives. This will require Air Force leaders to be willing to admit to political leadership that sometimes the US Air Force will be in a "can't-do" situation. Political and military leaderships together will have to recognize Clausewitz's observation that the choice of the military instrument inevitably will force change on the political objective. That change need not be drastic, but the recognition that change will be made needs to be understood. Political limits are a necessity, but military leaders must be ready to frankly admit it when such limits reduce the chances for success. Needed will be honest, clear recognition of the necessity for overall political direction, and conversely, honest, clear explanation of military capabilities within the bounds of such direction. Then, relying on air doctrine tempered with a sound appreciation of the situation, airpower can achieve its potential as a decisive element of modern warfare—at virtually any level of intensity.

# NOTES

1. Middleton, "Iran-Iraq Impasse," *NYT*, 6 October 1980, A14.

2. See comments on this treaty in Rouhollah K. Ramazani, *Iran's Foreign Policy, 1941–1973: A Study of Foreign Policy in Modernizing Nations* (Charlottesville: University Press of Virginia, 1975), 33–34, 300–1, for example.

3. Robert Bailey, "The War," *MEED* 24, no. 42 (17 October 1980): 15.

4. Milton, "Cauldron," 99.

5. Carl von Clausewitz, *On War*, edited and translated by Michael Howard and Peter Paret (Princeton, N.J.: Princeton University Press, 1976), 87.

6. Ibid.

7. "Iran's November Offensive Discussed," *JPRS Near East/North Africa Report*, 18 February 1981, 52. (Article in Paris newspaper *Al-Watan Al-'Arabi* in Arabic, no. 253, dated 18–24 December 1981, entitled "Iraqi Vigilance Aborts Blind 'Attack of Millions'.")

8. Clausewitz, 184–86.

9. Lt Col al-Haytham al-Ayoubi, *Middle East Crucible: Studies on the Arab-Israeli War of October 1973*, edited by Nasser H. Aruri (Wilmette, Ill.: The Medina University Press International, 1975), 85. A contemporary reference about the same aspect is found in Youssef M. Ibrahim, "Qualified Victory for Iraqis: Iran War in Low Gear," *NYT*, 10 December 1980, A13, in which an Arab diplomat in Baghdad was quoted as saying: "It really does not matter to Khomeini if the country's economy is run down, or if his army is wiped out . . . or even if half the country is occupied."

10. Warfare against Bedouin raiders employing these same tactics in Iraq in the 1920s is the bulk of the story in Sir John Bagot Glubb, *War in the Desert: An R.A.F. Frontier Campaign* (London: Hodder and Stoughton, 1960).

11. Majid Khadduri, *War and Peace in the Law of Islam* (Baltimore: Johns Hopkins University Press, 1955), 133–36.

12. See, for example, the studies of Middle Eastern war termination of Janice Gross Stein, "Proxy Wars: How Superpowers End Them: The Diplomacy of War Termination in the Middle East," *International Journal* 35, no. 3 (Summer 1980): 478–519; and Yaacov Bar-Siman-Tov, "Constraints and Limitations in Limited Local War: The Case of the Yom Kippur War," *Jerusalem Journal of International Relations* 5, no. 2 (1981): 46–61.

13. "Why Aren't the Iraqis Going for the Artery?" *The Economist* 277, no. 7154 (11 October 1980): 43–44.

14. Bernard Gwertzman, "Iran Is Said to Be Receiving Arms and Medicines from North Korea," *NYT*, 9 October 1980, 1; Mossberg, "N. Korea, Syria Is Helping Iran, US Sources Say," *WSJ*, 9 October 1980, 4.

15. "Navy Commander on Gulf Islands, War with Iraq," *FBIS-SAS-80-242*.

16. "Intelligence Limited," *AWST* 113 (13 October): 24.

17. el-Edroos, 422.

18. Ibid., 424.

19. Louise E. Sweet, "Camel Raiding of North Arabian Bedouin: A Mechanism of Ecological Adaptation," in *Peoples and Cultures of the Middle East, Volume I: Cultural Depth and Diversity*, edited by Louise E. Sweet (Garden City, N.Y.: Natural History Press, 1970), 165–289.

20. D. R. Hill, "The Role of the Camel and the Horse in the Early Arab Conquests," in *War, Technology, and Society in the Middle East*, edited by V. J. Parry and M. E. Yapp (London: Oxford University Press, 1975), 33–43.

21. Glubb.

22. Maj Gen Mohammad Gamal el-Din Mahfouz, "Lessons from the Great Battle of Badr," *Islamic Defence Review* 6, no. 1 (1981): 9–21.

# *Glossary*

| | |
|---|---|
| AAA | antiaircraft artillery |
| BAI | battlefield area interdiction |
| CAP | combat air patrol |
| CAS | close air support |
| $C^3$ | command, control, and communications |
| DASC | direct air support center |
| EAF | Egyptian Air Force |
| Fedayeen | literally "self-sacrificer," refers to Arab guerrillas |
| Hawk | Homing-All-the-Way-Killer (US SAM) |
| IIAF | Iranian Air Force |
| IQAF | Iraqi Air Force |
| IAF | Israeli Air Force |
| IFF | identification, friend or foe |
| LPG | liquified petroleum gas |
| MAP | Military Assistance Program |
| Mullah | Muslim (usually Shia) religious leader |
| OPEC | Organization of Petroleum Exporting Countries |
| RAF | Royal Air Force |
| ROTC | Reserve Officer Training Corps |
| SAM | surface-to-air missile |
| TOW | tube-launched, optically-tracked, wire-guided |
| Transjordan | the name of the state of Jordan prior to 1948 |
| US | United States |
| USAF | United States Air Force |
| USSR | Union of Soviet Socialist Republics |

# Bibliography

Abu Jaber, Kamel S. *The Arab Ba'th Socialist Party: History, Ideology, and Organization*. Syracuse, N.Y.: Syracuse University Press, 1966.

Adan, Avraham (Bren). *On the Banks of the Suez*. San Rafael, Calif.: Presidio Press, 1980.

Air Force Manual 1–1, *Functions and Basic Doctrine of the United States Air Force*. Washington, D.C.: Government Printing Office, 14 February 1979.

Air Force Manual 2–1, *Tactical Air Operations—Counter–Air, Close Air Support, and Air Interdiction*. Washington, D.C.: Government Printing Office, 2 May 1969.

Alexander, Yonah and Allan Nanes, eds. *The United States and Iran: A Documentary History*. Frederick, Md.: University Publications of America, 1980.

"Algiers Agreement Declared Null." *Middle East Economic Digest* 23, no. 38 (19 September 1980): 33.

Amos, John W., II. *Arab-Israeli Military/Political Relations: Arab Perceptions and the Politics of Escalation*. New York: Pergamon Press, 1979.

"Armies of Iran and Iraq Go on Alert as Baghdad Expels 7,000 Iranians." *Wall Street Journal*, 8 April 1980, 3.

"Arab Air Power, Part One." *Air International* 12 (June 1977): 275–81+.

"Arab Air Power, Part Four." *Air International* 13 (September 1977): 121–25+.

"Arab Air Power, Part Two." *Air International* 13 (July 1977): 7.

Aruri, Nasser H., ed. *Middle East Crucible: Studies on the Arab-Israeli War of October 1973*. Wilmette, Ill.: The Medina University Press International, 1975.

"As War Comes to Teheran, People Scurry to Stock Up." *New York Times*, 25 September 1980, A16.

el-Badri, Hassan, Taha el-Magdoub, Mohammed Dia el-Din Zohdy. *The Ramadan War, 1973*. Dunn Loring, Va.: T. N. Dupuy Assocs., Inc., 1978.

Bailey, Robert. "Iraq Covets Opponents' Weaponry." *Middle East Economic Digest* 24, no. 43 (24 October 1980): 7.

_____. "The Spectre of a Sudden Strike." *Middle East Economic Digest* 24, no. 44 (31 October 1980): 6–9.

_____. "The War." *Middle East Economic Digest* 24, no. 42 (17 October 1980): 15–21.

Bar-Siman-Tov, Yaacov. "Constraints and Limitations in Limited Local War: The Case of the Yom Kippur War." *Jerusalem Journal of International Relations* 5, no. 2 (1981): 46–61.

Beaufre, André. *The Suez Expedition 1956*. Translated by Richard Barry. New York: Frederick A. Praeger, Inc., 1969.

Be'eri, Eliezar. *Army Officers in Arab Politics and Society*. New York: Frederick A. Praeger, Inc., 1970.

Bill, James A'lban. "Iran and the Crisis of '78." *Foreign Affairs* 52, no. 2 (Winter 1978–1979): 323–42.

_____ . *The Politics of Iran: Groups, Classes and Modernization*. Columbus, Ohio: Charles E. Merrill Publishing Co., 1972.

Bird, David. "3 Americans Feared Dead in Air Raid on Iraqi Plant." *New York Times*, 25 September 1980, A13.

al-Bustany, Basil. "Iraq: Economic Developments." *AEI Foreign Policy and Defense Review* 2 (1980): 38–44.

Canby, Steven L. and Edward N. Luttwak. *The Control of Arms Transfers and Perceived Security Needs*. Prepared under contract #AC9WC112 by C&L Associates, Potomac, Md., for US Arms Control and Disarmament Agency, 14 April 1980.

Chubin, Shahram. "Iran's Security in the 1980s." *International Security* 2, no. 3 (Winter 1978): 51–80.

Clausewitz, Carl von. *On War*. Edited and translated by Michael Howard and Peter Paret. Princeton, N.J.: Princeton University Press, 1976.

Cordesman, Anthony H. "Lessons of the Iran-Iraq War: The First Round." *Armed Forces Journal International* 119 (April 1982): 32–47.

*Daily Report, Middle East and Africa*. Washington, D.C.: Foreign Broadcast Information Service.

*Daily Report, South Asia*. Washington, D.C.: Foreign Broadcast Information Service.

"Damage to Iran, Iraq Oil Facilities Feared Extensive." *Wall Street Journal*, 8 October 1980, 2.

Dawisha, Adeed I. "Iraq and the Arab World: The Gulf War and After." *The World Today* 37, no. 5 (May 1981): 188–94.

_____ . "Iraq: The West's Opportunity." *Foreign Policy*, Winter 1980-1981, 134–53.

Devlin, John F. *The Ba'th Party: A History from Its Origins to 1966*. Stanford, Calif.: Hoover Institution Press, 1976.

Dupuy, Col Trevor N. (US Army, Ret.) *Elusive Victory: The Arab-Israeli Wars, 1947–1974*. New York: Harper & Row, Publishers, Inc., 1978.

el-Edroos, Brig S. A. *The Hashemite Arab Army, 1908-1979: An Appreciation and Analysis of Military Operations*. Amman, Jordan: The Publishing Committee and Fakenham, Norfolk, U.K.: Fakenham Press, Ltd., 1980.

Fairhall, David. "The Iran-Iraq War at First Hand." *Defense Week* 1, no. 31 (3 November 1980): 4–5.

Fatemi, Khosrow. "Leadership by Distrust: The Shah's *Modus Operandi*." *Middle East Journal* 36, no. 1 (Winter 1982): 48–61.

Forbis, William H. *Fall of the Peacock Throne: The Story of Iran*. New York: Harper & Row, Publishers, Inc., 1980.

Fukuyama, Francis. *The Soviet Union and Iraq Since 1968*. Santa Monica, Calif.: Rand Corp. Note N-1524, July 1980.

Fullick, Roy and Geoffrey Powell. *Suez: The Double War*. London: Hamish Hamilton, 1979.

Geisenheyner, Stefan. "The Arab Air Forces: Will They Try Again?" *Air Force Magazine* 51 (July 1968): 44–48.

Glassman, Jon D. *Arms for the Arabs: The Soviet Union and War in the Middle East*. Baltimore: Johns Hopkins University Press, 1975.

Glubb, Sir John Bagot. *War in the Desert: An R.A.F. Frontier Campaign*. London: Hodder and Stoughton, 1960.

Graham, Robert. *Iran: The Illusion of Power*. New York: St. Martin's Press, 1979.

Griffiths, David R. "Iran Begins to Use Cobras, Mavericks." *Aviation Week and Space Technology* 113 (13 October 1980): 24–25.

Gwertzman, Bernard. "Iran Is Said to Be Receiving Arms and Medicines From North Korea." *New York Times*, 9 October 1980, 1.

Haggerty, Col J. J. "The Seeds of Qadisizah—The Iraqi-Iranian War." *Army Quarterly and Defence Journal* 111, no. 1 (January 1981): 37–43.

Halliday, Fred. "Interviews—Ba'th Command:'Initially We Were Happy to See the Fall of the Shah'." *MERIP Reports* 97, June 1981, 19–21.

Halloran, Richard. "British, in 1950, Helped Map Iraqi Invasion of Iran." *New York Times*, 16 October 1980, A15

_____ . "Iranians' Effectiveness in Fighting Iraq Is Astonishing U.S. Military Analysts." *New York Times*, 15 October 1980, A14.

_____ . "Iraq Said to Send Planes to Foreign Havens." *New York Times*, 3 October 1980, A10.

Heikal, Mohamed. *The Road to Ramadan*. New York: Ballantine Books, 1976.

Heller, Mark. "Politics and the Military in Iraq and Jordan, 1920–1958: The British Influence." *Armed Forces and Society* 4 (November 1977): 75–99.

Henriques, Robert. *A Hundred Hours to Suez: An Account of Israel's Campaign in the Sinai Peninsula*. New York: Viking Press, 1957.

Hershey, Robert D., Jr. "Iraq Halts Export of Its Oil as Result of Damage by Iran." *New York Times*, 27 September 1980, 1.

Hill, D. R. "The Role of the Camel and the Horse in the Early Arab Conquests." *War, Technology, and Society in the Middle East*. Edited by V. J. Parry and M. E. Yapp. London: Oxford University Press, 1975.

Howe, Marvine. "Iraqis Resume Pumping of Oil by Pipeline Across Turkey." *New York Times*, 21 November 1980, A14.

Hurewitz, J. C. *Middle East Politics: The Military Dimension*. New York: Frederick A. Praeger, 1969.

Hussein, Saddam. *Social and Foreign Affairs in Iraq*. Translated by Khalid Kishtainy. London: Croom Helm Ltd., 1979.

Ibrahim, Youssef M. "Iraq and Iran Battle for Key Cities; A War of Attrition Appears Likely." *New York Times*, 4 October 1980, 1.

_____ ."Qualified Victory for Iraqis: Iran War in Low Gear." *New York Times*, 10 December 1980, A13.

Ignatius, David. "Vignettes of War: Phantom and Taxi; Suspicion in Basra." *Wall Street Journal*, 3 October 1980, 1.

Insight Team of the *London Sunday Times, The Yom Kippur War*. Garden City, N.Y.: Doubleday & Co., Inc., 1974.

"In Teheran, Enforced Blackouts; In Baghdad, Lively Nonchalance: The War Is Hailed in Iraq." *New York Times*, 30 September 1980, 1.

"Intelligence Limited." *Aviation Week and Space Technology* 113 (13 October 1980): 24.

"Iranian/Iraqi Air Strikes Appear at 'Limited' Level." *Aviation Week and Space Technology* 113 (6 October 1980): 20–21.

"Iranians Bomb Dam in Iraq's Kurd Area." *New York Times*, 22 November 1980, 4.

"Iran-Iraq Clashes Intensify." *Middle East Economic Digest* 24, no. 37 (12 September 1980): 13.

"Iran-Iraq: Treaty on International Borders and Good Neighborly Relations." *International Legal Materials* 14 (September 1975): 1133–38.

"Iran's November Offensive Discussed." *Joint Publications Research Service Near East/North Africa Report*, 18 February 1981, 52.

"Iran Using F-14 in 'Mini-AWACS' Role." *Aerospace Daily* 105, no. 30 (14 October 1980): 236.

"Iraq Asks France for Crotale." *International Defense Intelligence Newsletter (DMS)*, 3 November 1980, 2.

"Iraq Ends 1975 Border Pact with Iran as Frontier Clashes Continue." *New York Times*, 18 September 1980, A8.

"The Iraqi Baath Party II." *Le Matin An-Nahar Arab Report 5* (11 November 1974).

"Iraqi SAMs." *Strategy Week* 7, no. 2 (19–25 January 1981): 1.

"Iraqis Negotiating Rapier Buy?" *International Defense Intelligence Newsletter (DMS)*, 22 December 1980, 3.

"Iraqis Want Roland." *International Defense Intelligence Newsletter (DMS)*, 30 March 1981, 3.

"Iraqi Tank Guns Stop Missile Helicopters." *Aviation Week and Space Technology* 113 (24 November 1980): 66.

"Iraq Using US AWACS Link; Iran Uses F-14." *Strategy Week* 6, no. 42 (20–26 October 1980): 5.

Keddie, Nikki R. *Iran: Religion, Politics and Society*. Totowa, N.J.: Frank Cass & Co. Ltd., 1980.

Khadduri, Majid. *Arab Contemporaries: The Role of Personalities in Politics*. Baltimore: Johns Hopkins University Press, 1973.

_____ . *Political Trends in the Arab World: The Role of Ideas and Ideals in Politics*. Baltimore: Johns Hopkins University Press, 1970.

_____ . *War and Peace in the Law of Islam*. Baltimore: Johns Hopkins University Press, 1955.

Kifner, John. "Amid Confusion of Battle, Iraqis Press On." *New York Times*, 28 September 1980, 1.

_____ ."Attacking Iraqi Troops in Iran Find the Foe Still Fights." *New York Times*, 1 October 1980, 1.

_____ ."Baghdad Says Its Troops Capture Khurramshahr and Cut a Rail Line." *New York Times*, 26 Septemer 1980, 1.

_____ ."Iranian Jets Said to Damage Several Iraqi Oil Plants." *New York Times*, 3 October 1980, A10.

_____ ."Iraqi Oil Center Damaged." *New York Times*, 30 September 1980, A14.

_____ ."Iraqi Planes Strike 10 Airfields in Iran; Oil Area Imperiled." *New York Times*, 23 September 1980, 1.

Kramer, Martin S. *Political Islam*. Beverly Hills/London: Sage Publications, 1980.

Lorch, Netanel. *The Edge of the Sword: Israel's War of Independence, 1947–1949*. New York: G. P. Putnam's Sons, 1961.

Love, Kennett. *Suez: The Twice-Fought War*. New York: McGraw-Hill, 1969.

Mahfouz, Maj Gen Mohammad Gamal el-Din. "Lessons from the Great Battle of Badr." *Islamic Defence Review* 6, no. 1 (1981): 9–21.

Marr, Phebe A. "Iraq: Sociopolitical Developments." *AEI Foreign Policy and Defense Review* 2 (1980): 30–38.

_____ ."The Political Elite in Iraq." *Political Elites in the Middle East*, ed. George Lenczowski. Washington, D.C.: American Enterprise Institute for Public Policy Research, 1975.

McLaurin, R. D.; Mohammed Mughisquddin; and Abraham R. Wagner. *Foreign Policy Making in the Middle East: Domestic Influences on Policy in Egypt, Iraq, Israel, and Syria*. New York: Praeger Publishers, 1977.

"Middle East: Iraq Accuses Syria." *Strategy Week* 7, no. 15 (20–26 April 1981): 2.

Middleton, Drew. "Air War's Emerging Role." *New York Times*, 9 October 1980, A16.

_____ . "Factor in Iraqi Push: Iranian Exiles' Aid." *New York Times*, 27 September 1980, 4.

_____ . "Iran-Iraq Impasse: Ground War Stalls, Yet Neither Side Exploits Air Power." *New York Times*, 6 October 1980, A14.

_____ . "Iraq Offensive in Slowdown?" *New York Times*, 29 September 1980, A13.

_____ . "Iraq's Waning Attack." *New York Times*, 2 October 1980, A16.

_____ . "Tactics in Gulf War." *New York Times*, 19 October 1980, 12.

"MiG-23 Draws Iraqi Complaints." *Strategy Week* 6, no. 41 (13–19 October 1980): 4.

"MiG-25s [sic] Equipped with Magic Missiles?" *International Defense Intelligence Newsletter (DMS)*, 8 June 1981, 3.

*The Military Balance 1980–1981*. London: International Institute for Strategic Studies, 1980.

Milton, T. R. "Where the Cauldron Boiled Over." *Air Force Magazine* 64, no. 1 (January 1981): 98–102.

Momyer, Gen William W. *Airpower in Three Wars*. Washington, D.C.: Government Printing Office, January 1978.

Moran, Theodore. "Iranian Defense Expenditures and the Social Crisis." *International Security* 3, no. 3 (Winter 1978–1979): 178–92.

Morrison, Wayne. "Iraq: Little Islam, Much Modernism." *Asiaweek* 6 (19 September 1980): 30–31.

Mossberg, Walter S. "N. Korea, Syria Are Helping Iran, U.S. Sources Say." *Wall Street Journal*, 9 October 1980, 4.

Naqvi, M. B. "Strategic Overview of the Iran-Iraq War." *Defense Journal* (Karachi, Pakistan) 6, no. 10 (1980): 11–20.

Neuman, Stephanie. "Security, Military Expenditures and Socioeconomic Development: Reflections on Iran." *Orbis* 22, no. 3 (Fall 1978): 569–94.

Nutting, Anthony. *No End of a Lesson: The Story of Suez*. New York: Clarkson N. Potter, Inc., 1967.

Nyrop, Richard F., ed. *Iraq: A Country Study*. Washington, D.C.: American University, 1979.

O'Ballance, Edgar. *The Arab-Israeli War, 1948*. London: Faber and Faber, Ltd., 1956.

_____ . "The Iraqi-Iranian War: The First Round." *Parameters* 11, no. 1 (March 1981): 54–59.

_____ . *The Kurdish Revolt: 1961–1970*. Hamden, Conn.: Archon Books, 1973.

_____ . *No Victor, No Vanquished: The Yom Kippur War*. San Rafael, Calif., and London: Presidio Press, 1978.

_____ . *The Third Arab-Israeli War*. Hamden, Conn.: Archon Books, 1972.

Pahlavi, Mohammad Reza Shah. *Answer to History*. New York: Stern and Day, 1980.

_____ . *Mission for my Country*. New York: McGraw-Hill Book Co., 1961.

Palit, Maj Gen D. K. *Return to Sinai: The Arab Offensive October 1973*. Dehra Dun and New Dehli: Palit and Palit Publishers, 1974.

Paul, Bill. "Iraq's Ambitions: Baghdad Seeks to Use Oil to Gain Influence, Shed Its Radical Image. *Wall Street Journal*, 4 June 1980, 1.

_____ . "Who is Real Hussein—the Genial Jekyll or Hideous Hyde?" *Wall Street Journal*, 13 June 1980, 1.

Povey, Terry. "Fighting to a Stalemate." *The Middle East* 74 (December 1980): 25–28.

Pranger, Robert J. and Dale R. Tahtinen. "American Policy Options in Iran and the Persian Gulf." *AEI Foreign Policy and Defense Review* 1, no. 2 (1979).

Prime, Frank J. "France Confirms Reports It Has Handed Over 4 Mirage Jets to Iraqis." *New York Times*, 2 February 1981, A6.

Ramazani, Rouhollah K. *Iran's Foreign Policy, 1941–1973: A Study of Foreign Policy in Modernizing Nations*. Charlottesville: University Press of Virginia, 1975.

Rondot, Phillipe. "Iran-Iraq War Evaluated by French Journalist." *Joint Publications Research Service Near East/North Africa Report* 2357 (1 July 1981): 14–25.

Rubin, Barry. "Iraq's Attack on Iran May Mean Less Than the Reasons Behind It." *Journal of Commerce*, 2 December 1980, 4.

_____ . *Paved with Good Intentions: The American Experience and Iran*. New York and Oxford: Oxford University Press, 1980.

Safran, Nadav. "Trial by Ordeal: The Yom Kippur War, October 1973." *International Security* 2, no. 2 (Fall 1977): 133–70.

Schiff, Zeev. "The Israeli: Air Force." *Air Force Magazine* 59, no. 8 (August 1976): 31–38.

el-Shazly, Lt Gen Saad. *The Crossing of the Suez*. San Francisco: American Mideast Research, 1980.

"Shipments of Oil to Mediterranean Stopped by Iraqis." *Wall Street Journal*, 29 September 1980, 2.

Sicherman, Harvey. "Reflections on 'Iran and Iraq at War'." *Orbis* 24, no. 4 (Winter 1981): 711–18.

Siddiqi, Brig Abdul Rahmen. "The Gulf War of Attrition." *Defence Journal* (Karachi, Pakistan) 6, no. 10 (1980): 1–10.

_____ . "The Gulf's Wanton War." *Defence Journal* (Karachi, Pakistan) 6, no. 11 (1980): 1–10.

SIPRI (Stockholm International Peace Research Institute), *The Arms Trade with the Third World*. New York: Humanities Press, 1971.

Smith, Harvey H., et. al. *Area Handbook for Iraq*. Washington, D.C.:Government Printing Office, 1969.

Sreedhar. "State of Iranian Armed Forces." *Strategic Analysis* 4, no. 3 (June 1980): 107–11.

Stein, Janice Gross. "Proxy Wars: How Superpowers End Them: The Diplomacy of War Termination in the Middle East." *International Journal* 35, no. 3 (Summer 1980): 478–519.

Stork, Joe. "Iraq and the War in the Gulf." *MERIP Reports* 97, June 1981, 3–18.

Sweet, Louise E. "Camel Raiding of North Arabian Bedouin: A Mechanism of Ecological Adaptation." *Peoples and Cultures of the Middle East, Volume I: Cultural Depth and Diversity*, edited by Louise E. Sweet. Garden City, N.Y.: Natural History Press, 1970.

Taal, Alieu B. S. "Wars and Religion." *New Zealand International Review* 6 (March-April 1981): 29–30.

Tanner, Henry. "Jordan Acts to Aid Iraq with Supplies for War with Iran." *New York Times*, 7 October 1980, 1.

_____ . "Khomeini Dismisses Truce Offer, Vowing a Fight 'to the End'." *New York Times*, 1 October 1980, 1.

Thapar, R. S. "Iran-Iraq Border Confrontation." *Strategic Analysis* 3, no. 5 (August 1979): 190–95.

_____ . "Iran-Iraq Conflict." *Strategic Analysis* 4, no. 2 (May 1980): 62–67.

Tomasek, Robert D. "The Resolution of Major Controversies between Iran and Iraq." *World Affairs* 139, no. 3 (Winter 1976–1977): 206–30.

"Too Hot to Handle." *The Middle East* 73 (November 1980): 10–16.

United States Congress. House. Committee on Intelligence Relations Report of a Study Mission Pursuant to House Resolution 315. *United States Arms Sales to the Persian Gulf*, 94th Cong., 1st sess., January 1976.

United States Congress. House. Committee on International Relations, Staff Survey Mission Report Pursuant to House Resolution 313. *United States Arms Policies in the Persian Gulf and Red Sea Areas: Past, Present, and Future*, 95th Cong., 1st sess., December 1977.

United States Congress. Senate. Committee on Foreign Relations, Subcommittee on Foreign Assistance. *US Military Sales to Iran*, 94th Cong., 2d sess., Staff Report, July 1976.

"U.S., Russian Weapons Vie in Mideast." *Aviation Week and Space Technology* 113 (29 September 1980): 27–28+.

van Crevald, Martin. *Military Lessons of the Yom Kippur War: Historical Perspectives.* Beverly Hills: Sage Publications, 1975.

"War Developments." *Aviation Week and Space Technology* 113 (20 October 1980): 31.£ 18 Septq 1980, A8.

"Why Aren't the Iraqis Going for the Artery?" *The Economist* 227, no. 7154 (11 October 1980): 43–44.

Wiskari, Werner. "Iraq Said to Gain Its Border Aims in Iran Conflict." *New York Times*, 20 September 1980, 1.

Wright, Claudia. "Implications of the Iran-Iraq War." *Foreign Affairs* 59 (Winter 1980–1981): 275–303.

_____ . "Iraq—New Power in the Middle East." *Foreign Affairs* 58 (Winter 1979–1980): 257-77.

_____ . "The Strong Men of the Arab World." *Maclean's* 93 (30 June 1980): 26.